Contents

Introduction 5
The First Hebrews 9
The Children of Israel 12
The Exodus 14
The Ten Commandments 16
In the Desert 18
The Promised Land 20
The Judges of Israel 22
Gideon the Judge 24
The Philistines 25
Samuel, Judge and Prophet 26
Appoint for Us a King 28
Saul, a Troubled King 30

The House of David 32
Solomon, King of Peace 34
The Seeds of Rebellion 36
The Kingdom Is Divided 38
Prophetic Voices 40
Elijah and Elisha 42
The House of Omri 44
A Time of Prosperity 46
Assyria the Conqueror 47
Israel Falls 48
Isaiah, Statesman and Prophet 50
King Hezekiah Rebels 52

Decline of Assyria 54
The Babylonian Empire 56
Jeremiah, Advocate of Peace 58
Judah Falls 60
Cyrus, King of Persia 62
The Exiles 63
The Samaritans 64
Rebuilding the Temple 66
The Spiritual Revival 68
The Story of Purim 70
Timeline–The Age of the Tanak 72

Alexander the Great 74
The Septuagint 76
Torah Prophetic History–Tanak 77
The Seleucids Rule Israel 78
The Reign of Antiochus IV 80
The Battle for Freedom 82
The Great Assembly 84
Pharisees and Sadducees 85
Civil War in Judea 86
Julius Caesar and the Jews 87
Herod the Cruel Becomes Ruler 88
Economic Prosperity 90
Masada, the Fortress 91

Contents

The Leaders of Judea — 92
Revolt in Judea — 94
Birth of Christianity — 95
The Zealots Resist — 96
Judea Is Defeated — 98
The Fall of Masada — 100
The Struggle for Survival — 102
Christianity Begins — 104
Gamaliel II — 105
Rabbi Akiva and the Mishnah — 106
A New Rebellion — 107
Bar Kochba's Revolt — 108

Judah HaNasi — 110
The Oral Tradition — 112
Yohanan and Simeon — 114
Roman Christianity — 115
The Gemara — 116
The Byzantine Empire — 118
Babylonian Jewry — 119
Rav and Samuel — 120
Rava and Abaye — 122
Rav Ashi — 124
The Jews of Arabia — 125
Islam Begins — 126
The Holy Wars — 128
Timeline–The Age of Learning — 130

The Gaonim — 132
The Karaites — 133
Saadia Gaon — 134
The Masorah — 135
The Golden Age — 136
The Khazars — 137
Samuel Ibn Nagrela — 138
Solomon Ibn Gabirol — 139
Isaac Hakohen Alfasi — 140
Judah Halevi — 141
Moses ben Maimon — 142
The Crusades — 144

Jewish Changes — 146
Rabbi Solomon ben Itzhak-Rashi — 147
The Tosafists — 148
Badges, Blood Libels, and Black Death — 149
Meir of Rothenburg — 150
Christians in Spain — 151
Nahmanides — 152
The Kabbalah — 153
The Marranos — 154
The Inquisition — 155
The Expulsion from Spain — 156
Timeline–The Age of Europe Begins — 158
The Jews Leave Spain — 160
Index — 161

Introduction

It all began about 4,000 years ago in the ancient city of Ur, in what is now Iraq. Divinely inspired, Abraham and his wife Sarah, the first patriarch and matriarch, began a saga that produced the best of times and the worst of times for their descendants–the Jews.

Understanding Jewish History records the many stories of the journey of the Jewish people through the annals of time. It is a history filled with triumphs and defeats, joys and tragedies, destruction and rebuilding, and lastly, Holocaust and rebirth. The countless struggles conferred a historic immortality on some individuals and places scattered through a myriad of kingdoms and countries.

From the beginning, the Jewish homeland, Israel, was at the crossroads of many civilizations and was dominated by powerful nations. Yet, despite the overpowering foreign influences, the Jewish people managed to survive as a national entity. Even in exile, they miraculously retained their cohesiveness and their peoplehood.

There never was any doubt about what they were fighting for or whether their obstinancy was worth the price. They fought to retain the right to worship as they pleased and to maintain their own unique way of life.

Unfortunately, for thousands of years Jews were not masters of their own history. Defeats, dispersions, and expulsions scattered them throughout the world. More than any other people they have been actors in historical theaters other than their own. As Jews and as foreigners they were dependent on the events, politics, poverty, prosperity, and personalities of the dominant power.

Mostly, and especially during the Middle Ages, Jews were the pawns on the chessboard of power politics. When their usefulness ended, they became as scapegoats to divert the masses from their misery and powerlessness.

The Text

Understanding Jewish History 1, is a short, immensely readable history of the Jewish people. It contains 98 one- and two-page historical essays, illustrated with colorful photographs, action maps, and explanatory charts. Each of the photographs is accompanied by a comprehensive caption which provides additional information.

Introduction

Timelines

Understanding Jewish History also contains six colorful, illustrated Timelines. They present a compact record of Jewish history extending from the patriarchs and matriarchs to the expulsion from Spain. Each two-page unit, is a stand-alone, three-dimensional panoramic display featuring dates, places, events, personalities, and Jewish scholarly texts. Its format enables the reader to grasp the continuity and flow of Jewish history as well as its position in the general history of the host country or geographical areas.

Chronology

The chronology for the early history of Israel is inexact and dates may vary by as much as five to ten years. The approximate dates given offer a reasonable compromise. The dates become more exact during the period of the Middle Ages and onward.

Understanding Jewish History: Part 2

Part 2 starts with the Renaissance and continues up to the Oslo Agreements between Israel and the Palestine Liberation Organization.

Aknowledgments

Numerous multitalented people have worked hard to bring *Understanding Jewish History* to life. They believed in the project and labored long and arduously, critiquing, editing, updating, and researching.

I wish to thank the following for their expert assistance. It is their sense, sensibility, sensitivity, and scholarship that have shaped the text.

Howard Adelman
Els Bendheim
Yaakov Elman
Robert Milch
Richard White

The final responsibility for any omissions, errors and mistakes is my own.

The First Hebrews / ca. 2000–1700 B.C.E.

Abraham and Sarah

The first great figure to appear on the stage of Jewish history was Abraham. Many centuries ago (about 1900 B.C.E.), according to the Bible, God told Abraham and his family to leave their native city of Ur and settle in a place that would become their new homeland. Because they crossed the river Euphrates on their journey to the Promised Land, people called them Hebrews (Ivrim, "those who came from the other side"), a name which has stayed with the Jews to the present day.

In the fertile land of Mesopotamia where Abraham and his wife, Sarah, grew up, a great civilization had developed. Its chief city, Ur, was a short distance from the Euphrates. Modern archaeologists, excavating on the site of this ancient city, have unearthed many of its wonders. It was a thriving market center, visited by merchants from near and far.

The people who lived there worshipped many different gods. Abraham believed that there could be only one God.

The Fertile Crescent

As we trace Abraham's journey on the map, we see that he first went to Haran, a flourishing city in the kingdom of Mari. His father and brothers settled there, but Abraham moved on. We are told how Abraham worshipped the one true God, and how God promised Abraham the land

THE FERTILE CRESCENT

The Near East is the region between the Mediterranean, Caspian, and Red Seas and the Persian Gulf. It is in general a barren, arid area. However, in the midst of this uninviting expanse lies a crescent-shaped region of fertile, watered land called the Fertile Crescent. It is in the Fertile Crescent that the first great civilization appeared and man made the transition from a hunter of food to an organized, systematic food producer.

of Canaan as a homeland for him and for all his descendants. With Sarah, his servants, his household goods, and his cattle, Abraham pressed on to the Promised Land. His journey covered 600 miles, through the rich lands that bordered the great Arabian desert; from Ur near the Persian Gulf, up to Haran and on to Canaan. Following this route carefully on the map, we can clearly see that it forms a crescent, whence comes the name "Fertile Crescent," by which this area is often called, to contrast it with the barren desert on which it borders.

The inhabitants of Canaan cultivated barley fields, fig trees, and date palms, and tended cattle and sheep. Some of their towns were strongly fortified with walls and towers, so that people could take refuge from the frequent attacks of the desert nomads who stormed across the river Jordan to steal cattle and raid storehouses.

Abraham in Canaan

Abraham settled in the hills of Canaan, where he was less exposed to attack and where the land seemed less desirable to the Canaanites. At Mamre, near Hebron, he pitched his black goatskin tents. Here Abraham raised his son and heir, Isaac; and here, eventually, he bought a piece of land from Ephron the Hittite, to bury his beloved wife, Sarah, in the cave of Machpelah.

The Bible relates that before Abraham died, he arranged for Isaac's marriage. He sent his servant Eliezer to Haran to seek a wife for Isaac from the family of Laban, his kinsman. Jacob, the son of Isaac, also sought a wife from among his distant kinsmen. After spending many years in the service of his uncle Laban, Jacob married

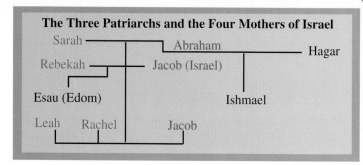

The Three Patriarchs and the Four Mothers of Israel

Sarah — Abraham — Hagar
Rebekah — Jacob (Israel)
Esau (Edom) — Ishmael
Leah — Rachel — Jacob

Excavation site of a temple in the ancient city of Ur.

King Ur-Nammu, the Sumerian king of Ur is standing in front of a plant, bringing an offering to an idol. The third dynasty of Ur was founded by Ur-Nammu. This carving was found on a stela.

Laban's two daughters, Rachel and Leah, who, together with their handmaids, bore him twelve sons.

Abraham, Isaac, and Jacob

Thus did the patriarchs, Abraham, Isaac, and Jacob, establish themselves in the land of Canaan. One of Jacob's contributions to his people was a new name for them. We are told that on his return to Canaan after serving his uncle Laban, Jacob met a man while crossing the river Jabbok. After wrestling with Jacob, the man revealed himself as an angel, a messenger of God. He gave Jacob the name of Israel, which means "he who struggled with God." Henceforth, Jacob's descendants were called the Children of Israel.

THE WORLD OF THE PATRIARCHS AND MATRIARCHS

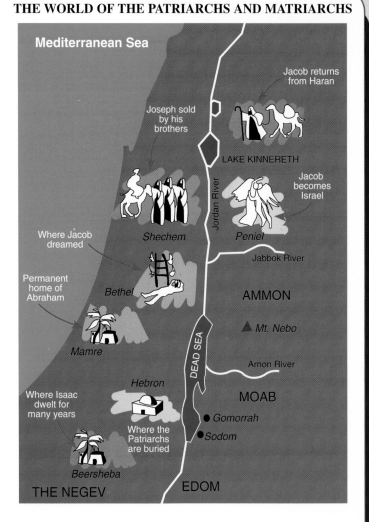

Mediterranean Sea

Jacob returns from Haran

Joseph sold by his brothers

LAKE KINNERETH

Jacob becomes Israel

Where Jacob dreamed

Shechem

Jordan River

Peniel

Jabbok River

Permanent home of Abraham

Bethel

AMMON

Mt. Nebo

Mamre

DEAD SEA

Arnon River

Hebron

Where Isaac dwelt for many years

MOAB

Gomorrah

Where the Patriarchs are buried

Sodom

Beersheba

THE NEGEV

EDOM

The Cave of Machpelah, where the patriarchs are buried, is behind the ancient walls of Hebron.

Hebron was David's capital until his conquest of Jerusalem. There was a Jewish community in Hebron during the Middle Ages and through the Turkish period. Hebron was ruled by Jordan from 1948 to 1967. It came under Israeli control during the Six-Day War, when the West Bank territories were conquered. In 1968 a new Jewish settlement called Kiryat Arba was established just outside of Hebron.

In 1995 as part of the peace agreement, the city of Hebron became a part of the Palestinian Authority.

The Children of Israel

The Hyksos in Egypt / ca. 1720–1600 B.C.E.

A time of famine came to Canaan, and the thoughts of Jacob-Israel turned longingly to the fertile land of the Nile, where food was plentiful even when other countries experienced famine. Joseph, one of Jacob's sons, was now living in Egypt, where he had risen from servitude to a position of great power, second in command only to the Pharaoh. At Joseph's invitation, Jacob brought his family and flocks into Egypt.

The Pharaoh assigned the territory of Goshen to the Israelites. It was good grazing land, and for many years the Israelites lived there in peace.

Modern historians believe that these events occurred about 1700 B.C.E., during the time when the Hyksos, a warlike tribe from Syria, swept into Egypt. The Hyksos ruled Egypt for about 120 years. Joseph was probably a high-ranking official under one of these powerful foreign rulers.

Slaves of Pharaoh / ca. 1290 B.C.E.

Eventually the Hyksos were defeated, and Egyptian kings once more ruled over the land. The new Pharaohs, as the Bible tells us, "did not know Joseph." No longer were the Israelites respected as the privileged descendants of a noble ancestor. Instead they were enslaved. Some historians believe that this took place during the reign of Rameses II (ca. 1290–1224 B.C.E.). Egypt

An Egyptian brick with the imprint of the seal of Rameses

was a growing empire and the new Pharaohs had great need for slaves to build their new cities and magnificent palaces.

Rameses feared an uprising among the slaves and took cruel precautions to prevent it. He issued a decree that all male children born to the Israelites must be killed. In this merciless way, Rameses hoped to keep the Israelites from growing in numbers.

Baby Moses

Soon after this decree was issued, a male child was born to Jochebed, an Israelite woman, and her husband Amram, of the tribe of Levi. Little did this couple dream that their son was destined to be known throughout the ages as one of the greatest leaders in history. Desperate to save the infant, they put him into a basket and set him afloat among the bulrushes of the Nile. He was found by an Egyptian princess while she and her handmaidens were bathing at the river.

A wall painting from about 1900 B.C.E. in an Egyptian tomb. This beautiful painting shows a group of Semites bringing gifts to the Egyptians.

Rameses II was most probably the Pharaoh who enslaved the Hebrews.

Earliest mention of Israel
The Egyptian text of two lines of Merneptah's stele, a transliteration, and a translation. After the word "Israel," note the figures of a man, a woman, and three straight lines.

The princess named him Moses, a name which means "drawn out of the water."

As a boy, Moses was given all the advantages enjoyed by members of Egypt's royal family. He may have learned to read and write on papyrus, a paperlike writing material which the Egyptians made from the leaves of the papyrus plant. Our word "paper" is derived from the name of this plant.

Fighting for Freedom
One day Moses was outraged to see an overseer beating an Israelite slave. Moses killed the overseer, and fled to the land of Midian in the Sinai desert. There he became a shepherd, living with a Kenite priest named Jethro. Moses married Jethro's daughter, Zipporah, who bore him two sons.

The Burning Bush
In the rugged mountains of Sinai, Moses had an inspiring experience. Through a vision of a Burning Bush that was not consumed, God told him to go down to Egypt, confront Pharaoh, and lead the Hebrew slaves to freedom. At first Moses refused, but eventually he accepted the responsibility. From that time forward, Moses was a man dedicated to the great task of leading his people to freedom. While the overseers lashed their weary bodies, Moses stirred their flagging spirits. The Israelites listened, and dared to dream of liberty and deliverance.

It was not an easy thing that Moses had chosen to do. Many obstacles were placed in his path by the Pharaoh, who according to some historians was Merneptah), the son of Rameses, who now sat on the throne of Egypt. Again and again Moses, with his brother Aaron, stood before him and pleaded for the Israelites' release. Pharaoh, full of confidence and power, turned a deaf ear to his pleas. But the burning sense of purpose that drove Moses on was more than a match for Pharaoh's stubbornness.

This scene of an overseer beating a slave was found in an Egyptian tomb.

The Exodus / ca. 1280 B.C.E.

Ten Plagues

Egypt had to be stricken by ten disastrous plagues before Pharaoh, fearing the wrath of the God whom Moses and his people worshipped, finally consented to release the Israelites and allow them to leave the land. A multitude of about 600,000 men together with women and children left Egypt on that memorable night of the Exodus. There was barely time to prepare the food they would need. The bread was so hurriedly baked that there was no time for the dough to rise. This was the origin of the custom of eating unleavened bread (matzot) on Passover (Pesach), the festival that commemorates the victory won for freedom so many centuries ago.

A group of wooden Nubian soldiers excavated from the tomb of an Egyptian prince. Such models were placed in tombs in the belief that they would serve the owner in the afterworld.

The Exodus: A March to Freedom / ca. 1280 B.C.E.

So the great march out of Egypt began, with families gathered together, each with its own tribe, twelve tribes in all. However, after begging the Israelites to leave, Pharaoh suddenly changed his mind and sent his charioteers to bring the slaves back. According to the Bible, Moses did not dare lead them by the established route, which was dangerously near Egypt's border forts, where soldiers might have attempted to prevent their escape. Instead, the great throng of people, young and old, carrying their meager belongings, marched slowly eastward to avoid the border posts.

Then their march was halted suddenly by an obstacle that seemed to be insurmountable. Silent and disheartened they stood, the light of hope slowly fading from their eyes as they gazed at the vast expanse of water before them. They had come to the end of dry land, to the shores of the Sea of Reeds (Yam Suf), the Suez arm of the Red Sea.

Bust of Merneptah (1235–1227 B.C.E.), son of Rameses II. Some historians believe that he was the Pharaoh of the Exodus.

Those who looked back in the direction of their former homes were greeted by a sight that chilled their already sinking hearts. Bearing down upon them was a column of Egyptian soldiers. With the sea before them and the army of Pharaoh closing in from behind, the Children of Israel were trapped.

Then, miraculously, a strong easterly wind arose. It drove back the ebbing waters of the sea, making a path of dry land. With joyful hearts, the throng followed Moses to the opposite shore. In fierce pursuit, Pharaoh's soldiers also took the dry path through the Sea of Reeds, but the wind turned and the tide rolled in. Back rushed the waters, engulfing the chariots and drowning the soldiers.

Free at Last

The Bible tells how the Israelites rejoiced when they found themselves safely across

This picture of Pharaoh Tutankhamen in his chariot was found in his tomb. The chariot reins are tied around the pharaoh's waist, freeing his arms and enabling him to shoot his arrows. The Bible describes the pursuit of the Israelites by the "chariot of the king of Egypt."

the sea. Moses composed a poem of praise to God. The women danced joyously to the music of their timbrels and sang a song composed by Miriam, Moses' sister.

Ahead of them lay untold dangers, but on this great day there was but one song in the hearts of the Israelites—a song of gratitude for their newly-won freedom.

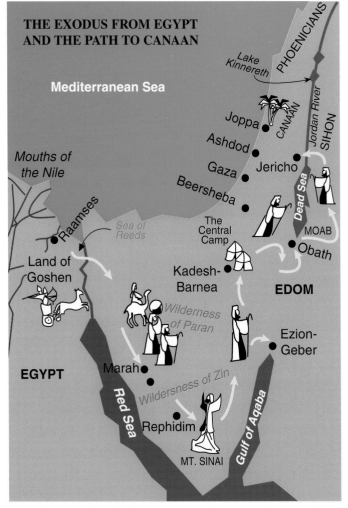

THE EXODUS FROM EGYPT
AND THE PATH TO CANAAN

According to the Bible, the Israelites left Egypt and traveled along the northern coast of the Sinai peninsula. During the forty years of wandering they passed through many kingdoms and endured great hardships.
The Israelites spent much time at the oasis of Kadesh-Barnea. Moses sent 12 spies into Canaan from this oasis.
At Marah the Israelites found bitter water. According to the Bible God showed Moses a plant which made the water drinkable.
Before the Israelites reached Mount Sinai, they battled the Amalekites at Rephidim.

Miriam and the Israelite women dancing with joy after their liberation from Egypt. This painting is from the Sarajevo Haggadah.

The Ten Commandments

Mount Sinai / ca. 1280 B.C.E.

When the Israelites reached Mount Sinai, Moses ordered them to pitch their tents. Here occurred the most important moment in Jewish history.

After the camp had been made, Moses ascended the mountain. For days, he was hidden from the people. Then, amidst thunder and lightning so intense that the very mountains shook, the voice of God reverberated throughout, proclaiming the Ten Commandments.

The Ten Commandments

Descending from the mountain, Moses brought down the Ten Commandments, carved upon two tablets of stone.

The Ten Commandments sealed a covenant between the young nation of

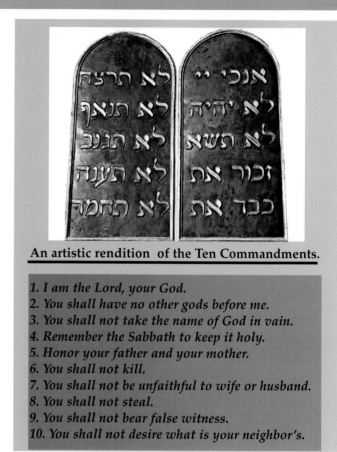

An artistic rendition of the Ten Commandments.

1. I am the Lord, your God.
2. You shall have no other gods before me.
3. You shall not take the name of God in vain.
4. Remember the Sabbath to keep it holy.
5. Honor your father and your mother.
6. You shall not kill.
7. You shall not be unfaithful to wife or husband.
8. You shall not steal.
9. You shall not bear false witness.
10. You shall not desire what is your neighbor's.

Israel and the one God. No other nation had a code of laws so just and humane. The Israelites now truly abandoned the ways of Egypt and dedicated themselves to live by this lofty code.

The Torah

According to tradition, the entire Torah was revealed to Moses on Mount Sinai. The Torah, also known as the Five Books of Moses, recounts the early history of the Jewish people and lays down the rules, laws, and ethical teachings of Judaism.

The Torah scroll used in the synagogue is written on parchment by a scribe in ancient Hebrew letters. As in days gone by, it is written with a feather pen and specially prepared ink.

In traditional synagogues the Torah is read aloud at services on Sabbaths, holy days, and Monday and Thursday mornings.

Moses bringing down the Ten Commandments. From the Sarajevo Haggadah.

Since the Torah is divided into 54 sections called Sidrot, it can be read through from beginning to end in one year, at the rate of one section a week (except for two weeks when two sections are read).

The Tabernacle

In order to provide a place where the Israelites could worship God, Moses appointed two craftsmen, Bezalel and Oholiab, to construct a sanctuary.

The sanctuary was designed to be portable. It was a constant reminder to the Israelites of their allegiance and dedication to the service of God. The primary structure was the Tent of Meeting, a large tent with a strong wooden frame. It consisted of an outer court, supported by pillars, and an inner court, separated from the outer court by curtains. In the inner court stood the Tabernacle. This was divided by a curtain or veil into the Holy Place, where the priests would offer sacrifices on the altar, and the Holy of Holies, which contained the Ark of the Covenant. The Holy of Holies symbolized God's mysterious presence.

The Torah vividly describes the Ark of the Covenant in which the two holy tablets brought down by Moses were kept. The Ark was a precious, portable shrine made of acacia wood, with handles for carrying it from place to place. Atop it were two carved angels called cherubim. The Ark and the holy objects used for the service in the Tabernacle were all fashioned by Bezalel.

Aaron and the Priesthood

Moses consecrated Aaron and his sons for the priesthood, anointing their heads with oil in a sacred ceremony. Forever after, Aaron, his sons, and their descendants were to be the priests (kohanim), of Israel. The duties of the priests were many and varied. Most important, they offered sacrifices for the people and raised their voices in prayer. The priestly garb was prescribed in the Torah. For Aaron, the high priest, it included a breastplate bearing the Urim and Tumim, twelve precious stones in four rows, each stone symbolizing one of the tribes of Israel. The high priest wore these garments when he stood before God in prayer.

The Torah describes the clothing and ornaments worn by the high priest. The Urim and Tumim were worn on the priest's chest. It was inlaid with 12 different stones, one for each of the tribes of Israel.

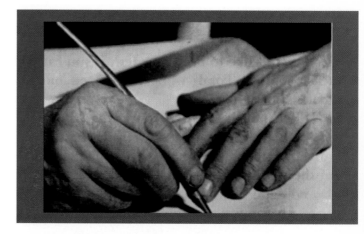

A *sofer*, or scribe, writing a Torah in the traditional way with a feather pen and special ink. In Babylonia, the Torah was divided into 54 sections called Sidrot, so that the entire Torah could be completely read in one whole year. In traditional synagogues the Torah is read on Sabbaths, holy days, and Monday and Thurday mornings.

In the Desert / ca. 1280–1240

The Wandering Begins

It was at Sinai that the Israelites first began to observe the laws and religious rituals laid down in the Torah. When the Israelites broke camp and continued their wanderings, they carried with them the Tent of Meeting and the Ark of the Covenant which housed the tablets of the law.

The Israelite wanderers were sincerely dedicated to the new ideals set forth in the Torah. The memory of the Exodus and the courage of their leaders, Moses, Aaron, and Miriam, was ever before them, inspiring them to renewed faith and purpose.

Scouting Canaan

At long last the Israelites drew close to the Promised Land. Moses gave the order for the march to halt, for he wanted time to map his strategy for the conquest of Canaan. Scouts were sent across the border, among them Caleb and Joshua, Moses' able young assistants. The scouts were ordered to find out all they could about the condi-

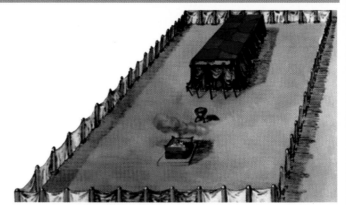

A reconstruction of the court of the Tabernacle. The large structure is the Tabernacle. In the center of the court is a laver so that the priests could wash their offerings. The altar for the offering is at the other end of the court.

tion of the land, the number of troops, and the strength of the fortifications. The scouts returned with conflicting reports. Some of them spoke in glowing terms of the land's fertility, bringing back luscious fruits as proof. Others spoke in more somber terms of well-armed soldiers and well-fortified cities.

The Years of Wandering

Moses realized that the Israelites lacked the faith and courage necessary for a successful invasion. He led them back into the desert, where they wandered for the next 40 years.

The Torah records the many difficulties the Israelites encountered during this time of wandering. Hunger and thirst stalked their path. Hostile desert tribes were a constant danger, harassing the people by day, and terrifying and robbing them by night.

The New Generation

At the end of 40 years of desert life, a new generation had grown to adulthood. Few remained of the generation who had known the chains of Egyptian slavery. The new generation had lived

The nomadic nature of the Israelite wanderings in the desert made it necessary to build a portable sanctuary for the Holy Ark in which the Ten Commandments were kept. The Book of Exodus describes its construction. It was 45 by 15 feet and was constructed of acacia wood. As pictured, the completed Tabernacle was draped with protective curtains.

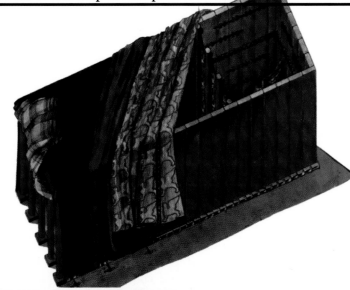

The Torah is divided into 5 books. The Hebrew and Latin titles are:

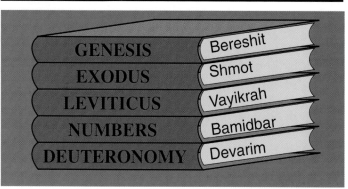

GENESIS — Bereshit
EXODUS — Shmot
LEVITICUS — Vayikrah
NUMBERS — Bamidbar
DEUTERONOMY — Devarim

no other life than that of the desert and had known no other gods but the one God, no other laws but the laws of the Torah.

Joshua Succeeds Moses

Moses, the great leader, grew old. The time had come to choose someone to take his place after he was gone. Moses' choice fell on Joshua, a man respected by the people and possessing a gift for military strategy. Into Joshua's capable hands Moses placed the task of invading Canaan.

The Death of Moses

Moses knew that he would not live to enter the Promised Land. After he had blessed and consecrated Joshua for his new responsibilities, Moses felt his work was done. From atop Mount Nebo he bade his people farewell. Then the old man gazed out over the rich and fertile land which stretched for miles beyond the mountain.

"This land," God told him, "which I swore to give to Abraham, Isaac, and Jacob, I will now give to your offspring."

"I have let you see it, but you shall not cross into it," ends the account of Moses' life. The Torah records his death with the phrase, "No one knows his burial place to this day."

There would be other great leaders in the years to come, but that unique and special era in their history through which Moses had guided them enshrined him in the hearts of Jews for all time.

From atop Mount Nebo Moses saw the land of Canaan, which God promised to give to the Children of Israel.

The Promised Land

The Invasion Begins / ca. 1240 B.C.E.

When Joshua decided the time was right for entering the Promised Land, he sent his officers through the great throng of Israelites encamped near the river Jordan. The officers instructed the people to prepare themselves. When they saw the Ark of the Covenant being carried across the river by the priests, they broke camp and followed.

The peoples of Canaan—the Canaanites, Jebusites, and Hittites—lived on farms and in fortified towns and cities. The houses of the city dwellers were of stone, and many of the cities were surrounded by strong walls and watchtowers. The tools these people used and their weapons of war were much more advanced than those of the Israelites. Their spears were tipped with iron, a new metal not yet widely used. They even had chariots, drawn by fine, swift horses. The Israelites, on the other hand, used simple spears and bows.

The Fall of Jericho / ca. 1225 B.C.E.

The Hebrew tribes crossed the Jordan near the Dead Sea and took the key city of Jericho, "whose walls came tumbling down." Thereafter, in a series of battles the Israelites captured the fortified cities of Lachish, Ai, Eglon, and many others.

The conquest of Canaan was accomplished by a spectacular invasion in which the Israelite defeated 31 kings. Joshua's campaign employed a series of brilliant maneuvers and surprise attacks.

Many of the Canaanites were panic-stricken by the Israelite onslaught. Six kings from the north joined forces to oppose the Israelite army. So Joshua and his men attacked the combined armies at the Waters of Meron and defeated them.

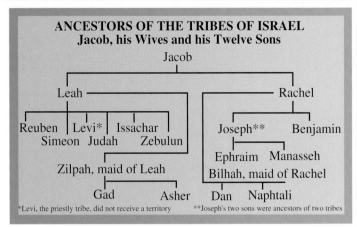

ANCESTORS OF THE TRIBES OF ISRAEL
Jacob, his Wives and his Twelve Sons

*Levi, the priestly tribe, did not receive a territory   **Joseph's two sons were ancestors of two tribes

TRIBAL SYMBOLS AND TERRITORIES

Note that the tribes of Gad, Reuben, and half of Manasseh were allotted territories on the other side of the Jordan River.

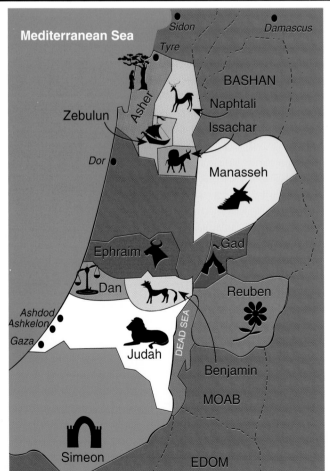

The Israelites Settle Canaan / ca. 1225 B.C.E.

As the conquest of Canaan proceeded, Joshua distributed the land among the Israelite tribes. He assigned portions to all of them except Levi, which was allotted 48 special cities in the territories of the other tribes. The Levites (and the priests, who were members of Levi) had the special assignment of administering the laws of Israel and tending the sanctuary which Joshua had established in Shiloh, where the Holy Ark and the Tabernacle were kept.

It was to Shiloh that the people made pilgrimages, bringing sacrifices and praying there together. The sanctuary was tended by Aaron's son Elazar and grandson Phinehas, assisted by the Levites. Other Levites traveled through the land, making the people familiar with the Torah and instructing them in the worship of the one God.

Israel's Greatest Threat

The gravest threat facing the Israelites was not the superiority of their enemies' weapons nor even the strong walls around their enemies' cities. It was a threat far more difficult to avoid and overcome, a threat to the very foundations of the faith of Israel. Upon entering Canaan, the Israelites found themselves mingling with peoples who worshipped idols.

Fearing that they would fall into the idolatrous ways of their pagan neighbors, Joshua, now an old man and knowing that his death was near, called the twelve tribes together for a great assembly at Shechem, near Shiloh. Gathered together before their leader, the people listened as Joshua impressed upon them the importance of remaining united and faithfully following the laws of the one God.

The people made a solemn promise to put away all the idols and hold steadfast to the Torah. With one voice they cried: "We will obey none but the God of Israel."

The excavations at biblical Shechem have uncovered this 12th century B.C.E. stone monument. Shechem was in the territory allotted to the tribe of Ephraim. Here, Joshua gave his farewell address and formally renewed the covenant made by the Israelites at Sinai.

A Canaanite shrine uncoverd at Hazor, 14th–13th century B.C.E. Note the hands reaching upwards to a disc and crescent, symbols of the Canaanite religion. The city, was a Canaanite stronghold. It was destroyed by Joshua but was later rebuilt by King Solomon.

The Judges of Israel / ca. 1225–ca. 1020 B.C.E.

After Joshua's death, the Israelites were guided by leaders called judges. Both men and women served as judges; among them were warriors, priests, and seers. The first judges led the Israelites in defense against the warlike pagan neighbors who frequently attacked their farms and towns. In times of peace the judges settled disputes and provided religious inspiration.

In periods when there was no judge representing a central authority for all Israel, some of the tribes would fall away from the laws given at Sinai. They would no longer make pilgrimages to the Tabernacle at Shiloh, but would take sacrifices to the Canaanite shrines and lay their offerings before the idols.

The Canaanite Threat

During the centuries after Joshua there were twelve judges. No longer half-starved desert nomads, the Israelites had now become farmers, shepherds, artisans, and city dwellers. Their new way of life, however, was beset with dangers from all sides. Canaanite soldiers often raided Israelite farms and storehouses. Though the Israelites bravely fought off the attackers, their efforts were futile against the armed might of Jabin, the most powerful Canaanite king. Jabin's army, commanded by his general, Sisera, was well-trained and

A Canaanite victory celebration on an ivory plaque. The ruler sits on his throne as a court musician plays a lyre. Behind the musician is a warrior leading two prisoners and an armored chariot.

equipped with heavy iron chariots and weapons.

Deborah, Leader and Judge / ca. 1100 B.C.E.

In the hill country of Ephraim lived a female judge named Deborah. People came from far and near to consult her. Deborah held court near her home at a place between Ramah and Bethel. Here she would sit beneath a palm tree and the people would come and tell her their problems.

Deborah resolved that Jabin must be defeated. When the time was ripe, she gathered her allies. Summoning Barak, an able warrior from the tribe of Naphtali, she ordered him to muster every available Israelite soldier and prepare to attack.

Together, Deborah and Barak led the warriors of Israel up the sides of Mount Tabor, a mountain that rises over the great plain of Jezreel near the Kishon River.

JUDGES

The twelve Judges of Israel whose histories are told in the Book of Judges:*

OTHNIEL	DEBORAH	JAIR	ELON
EHUD	GIDEON	JEPHTHAH	ABDON
SHAMGAR	TOLA	IBZAN	SAMSON

*The lives of the later judges, Eli and Samuel, are told in the Book of Samuel, I.

Mount Tabor, where Deborah and Barak defeated the Canaanite general Sisera.

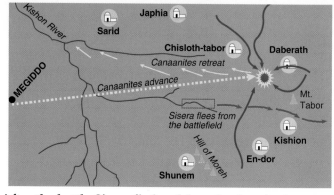

After the battle Sisera fled and found refuge in the tent of Jael.

Victory at Mount Tabor

Confident of an easy victory over this small army equipped with inferior weapons, the mighty King Jabin and his general, Sisera, assembled their troops and their iron chariots and waited beneath Mount Tabor for the Israelites to strike.

Shouting their battle cry, the Israelite warriors charged down the mountain and attacked the Canaanites. In the midst of the battle the skies opened and rain poured down. The Kishon, normally a quiet stream, became a raging torrent, rolling and rushing across the plain. The heavy iron wheels of Sisera's chariots were mired in thick, slippery mud. Weighed down by their heavy armor, the Canaanite solders were no match for the lightly armed Israelites, who seemed to be everywhere at once with lightning speed, cutting down the enemy right and left with their spears and slings.

Complete Victory

The Canaanites fled in utter confusion. Sisera, their general, sought refuge in the tent of Jael, a Kenite woman, begging her for water to quench his thirst. Jael gave the great warrior a dry cloak and some milk to drink, then stood guard at the door of the tent. Unaware that Jael and her husband,

Heber, were secret allies of the Israelites, Sisera thought himself safe and fell into a deep sleep. And while he slept, Jael slew him. According to the Book of Judges, Jael took a sharp tent peg, quietly crept close to the sleeping Sisera, then hammered it through his temples.

Deborah's Song

Great was the rejoicing of the Israelites when they learned that Sisera was dead and that the fierce Canaanite warriors had fled in confusion. Deborah, the prophetess who had so fearlessly led her people, sang a song of praise to God.

With the Israelite victory at Mount Tabor, the power of the Canaanites came to an end. The successful conquest of this troublesome enemy gave the Israelites a much firmer hold on their new land. Peace had come to the Promised Land—at least for a time.

A Canaanite clay altar excavated from the city of Tanach. It is dated to the 10th century B.C.E.

Gideon the Judge / ca. 1120 B.C.E.

New Enemies

Out of the east, from across the Jordan, came the Midianites, greedily searching for new grazing grounds and plunder. These desert raiders, warlike and strong, came riding on camels. Borne by the swift ships of the desert, the ruthless Midianites bore down on the land of Canaan, shattering the peaceful existence of the Israelites.

Gideon Fights Back

Once more a leader rose from the ranks of Israel to meet the challenge to freedom. The new leader was Gideon, a farmer from Ophrah. When he called for volunteers to battle the Midianites, the response was immediate. Thousands of Israelites came, but Gideon only chose the 300 most stalwart and God-fearing of them for a surprise attack.

In the dead silence of night the Israelite warriors stealthily approached the camp of the sleeping Midianites. Gideon's small army was equipped with odd weapons— burning torches, jars and pitchers. At a given signal, they held their torches high, shattering the jars and pitchers at the same time in one tremendous crash. The noise was deafening and, to add to the confusion, some of the Israelites blew their rams' horns, shouting, "For God and for Gideon!"

The Midianites were terrified. They tumbled from their tents and fled into the night. The Israelites pursued them and drove them out of the land. Never again did the Midianites attack Israel.

Gideon, a valiant warrior and brilliant strategist, was also a dynamic political leader. In his effort to defeat the Midianites he succeeded in reuniting the tribes of Israel.

God Shall Rule

So great was the people's confidence in Gideon and so sincere their love for him that the elders of the tribes asked him to be their king. To this request Gideon answered, "I shall not rule over you, neither shall my son rule over you. Only God shall rule over you."

Gideon served as judge in Israel for many peaceful years and died a very old man.

The Gezer Calendar Stone was discovered by R. Macalister in 1908. This 10th century B.C.E. limestone plaque is inscribed with the planting schedule of the ancient Palestinian farmer.

1 (Its?) months of ingathering 2 months of sow-
2 ng 2 months of late sowing
3 The month of pulling flax
4 The month of barley harvest
5 The month when everything else is harvested
6 2 months of vine-pruning
7 The month of summer fruit

The Philistines

Dangerous Neighbors / ca. 1200 B.C.E.

A time of great peril came upon the Israelites. Their most formidable enemies, the Philistines, were on the march.

The Philistines had come from far away. Their long trek had led them through Crete, across the Aegean Sea by ship and through Asia Minor on foot and by oxcart. Wherever they passed, they left a trail of pillage and bloodshed in their wake. Their ambitious plan of conquest even included mighty Egypt.

The Philistines

The Philistines marched into Canaan victoriously, for the inhabitants were helpless before them. They conquered the rich coastal cities and established five powerful city-states: Ashkelon, Ashdod, Ekron, Gaza, and Gath. Each of these cities in the southern part of the fertile coastal plain was ruled by an independent Philistine prince, but all five were united as allies in peace and in war. Next the Philistines began to subject the land of Israel to their power. They drove the tribe of Dan out of its territory. The Danites were forced to move on and settle in the far north of the land.

Samson, Man of Strength / ca. 1100 B.C.E.

By the time of Samson, the last of the judges, Israel was desperately trying to hold off the Philistines. Samson's great physical strength was known and admired by both Philistines and Israelites. The story of how this fearless hero was finally brought down by the trickery and deceit of his Philistine sweetheart, Delilah, has been made famous in the world's music and literature. During a Philistine festival, Samson, blinded and in chains, was exhibited at Gaza. Sightless and alone, he exerted the last of his remaining strength to bring down a great Philistine temple, destroying many of his captors and perishing under the crashing pillars himself.

This drawing from an Egyptian stone relief pictures the naval engagement between the ships of Rameses III and the Philistines.

A stone relief from Thebes showing a group of Philistine prisoners of Rameses III. In hieroglyphics, the Philistines were called *peles et*. The name Palestine was derived from this word.

Samuel, Judge and Prophet / ca. 1040–1020 B.C.E.

The Birth of Samuel

In the period after Samson's death, the sanctuary at Shiloh was tended by Eli, who served as both priest and judge.

Eli noticed that a woman named Hannah was a frequent visitor to the sanctuary at Shiloh. When the kindly priest learned that Hannah was there to pray for the birth of a son, he comforted her and told her to be of good faith, promising that God would answer her prayer. Soon thereafter a son was born to Hannah. She called the child Samuel (from the Hebrew *shama el*, "God heard").

A Future Leader

As soon as Samuel was old enough to leave home, Hannah brought him to Shiloh. She asked Eli to make the boy his assistant in the service of God. The priest was delighted to grant Hannah's request, and Samuel proved an apt and eager pupil.

Eli was very pleased with Samuel, for the youngster seemed truly worthy to be a future leader and judge of Israel, even though he was not a descendent of the priestly family of Aaron. Eli instructed Samuel in the ways of the Torah and the faith of Israel.

As the years passed, Hannah's son became well known for his knowledge and great wisdom. In time he was revered as a man of divine inspiration, a judge and a prophet in Israel. Samuel became the national leader and head of the tribes.

The Battle of Aphek

Meanwhile, the Philistines, Israel's dreaded foes, had grown increasingly powerful. At last, the Philistine and Israelite armies met in a bloody battle on the plain of Aphek. The Israelites suffered heavy losses. In desperation, the elders of the tribes went to Eli.

"Let us carry the Holy Ark into battle," they pleaded. "It will inspire us to victory."

With the Holy Ark in their midst, the Israelites fought a brave fight, but the superior arms and training of the Philistines proved overwhelming.

The Holy Ark of the Covenant, with the tablets of the law, was captured by the enemy.

Philistines, Masters of Israel

The Philistines had become masters in the land. They destroyed the sanctuary at Shiloh, and the priests and Levites scattered to different parts of the country.

Samuel's task of keeping alive the faith of Israel was not an easy one in those dark days. Fear and discouragement lay like a

Archaeologists have unearthed the stone relief of the Holy Ark in the ancient synagogue in Capernaum. The original Holy Ark was built by Moses, and was carried from place to place before being permanently enshrined in the First Temple.

heavy yoke upon the people. They were forced to pay heavy tribute to the Philistines. They were not permitted to carry weapons, and their pickaxes and plowshares had to be sharpened in the forges of the overlords.

All Israelites were forbidden to use iron, the precious new metal, for it was to be forged only in the cities of the Philistines. Many Israelites turned away from God in bitterness and began to worship Baal and Astarte, the gods of their pagan conquerors.

However, in the midst of utter despair and defeat, the Israelites won a victory of sorts. The Philistines were afflicted by a terrible plague. Convinced that it was a punishment for having taken the Ark of the Covenant, the enemies of Israel returned it to the Israelites.

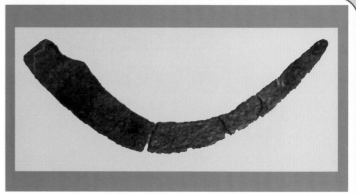

An ancient iron sickle. This sharp knife was used for harvesting grain. Sickles are still used in underdeveloped regions of the world.

The Ark in the Land of the Philistines. Taken from the fresco in the synagogue at Dura-Europos, 3rd century, C.E.

A 13th century French manuscript depicts the Ark of the Covenant being brought out. The Ark of the Covenant was a gold-plated chest in which the Ten Commandments given by God to Moses were stored. It was originally kept at Shiloh, and brought out during battles to encourage the army.

King Solomon placed the Ark of the Covenant in the Holy of Holies, of the Temple at Jerusalem. It disappeared after the destruction of the Temple in 586 B.C.E.

Appoint for Us a King

Voices of Hope

Samuel realized that if Israel was to survive, its people had to be united and inspired. Like the priests and Levites of earlier times, he began traveling through the land, encouraging the people everywhere to hold fast to their faith.

On his travels, Samuel attracted many followers, men who were uplifted by his words and, like himself, felt called upon to talk to the people about God and hope. Samuel's disciples would sing and play the harp, telling the stories of Israel's past and expounding the laws of the Torah.

Idol worship was popular among some of the Israelites. The prophet Samuel and his followers traveled throughout the land encouraging the people to hold true to their faith.

This impression of a Canaanite seal found at Bethel shows the idol Baal and his wife Ashtoreth. The name Ashtoreth is written in Egyptian characters in the center of the seal. Ashtoreth is mentioned several times in the Bible.

"Appoint Us a King"

When Samuel grew old, the elders of the tribes became fearful about the future. The tribes were worn out by the constant warfare with their enemies. They felt the need for a central authority which could mold them into a unified strong nation. The people appealed to Samuel, "Appoint us a king who will rule us, like the other nations." Samuel was deeply troubled when the tribal elders asked him to select a king to rule over them. The wise old judge was well-versed in the laws of Israel and knew the needs of a Israeli society.

Samuel's Leadership / ca. 1040–1010 B.C.E.

Samuel realized that life under a king would be different in many ways. The people would have to maintain a grand style of living for the king. A king would require a royal palace and servants. Hitherto the people had defended the land of their own free will, but with a king a regular army would be needed, with men from each tribe to guard and serve him. Taxes would be levied to meet the government's civil and military expenses. One by one, Samuel

presented these arguments against the establishment of a kingdom, but the elders refused to be discouraged. The people had set their hearts on having a king. Reluctantly Samuel bowed to their wishes.

Saul, Israel's First King / ca. 1020–1004 B.C.E.

Under God's guidance, Samuel chose the first king of Israel with great wisdom and much diplomacy. Because of the competition and rivalry among the more powerful tribes, Samuel turned to the smaller, poorer tribe of Benjamin. By selecting a man from the tribe of Benjamin, Samuel wisely avoided the danger of setting the great rival tribes against one another. The man chosen by Samuel was Saul, who was respected by all and a valiant fighter.

The Bible tells how Saul left home to go in search of his father's runaway donkeys. Traveling through Zuph, he stopped to ask the advice of Samuel, who was speaking there to the people. Samuel took Saul into the hills, where he told the young man that instead of the donkeys which he had gone to seek, he had found a crown.

King Saul's Victory

Saul soon proved himself a forceful leader. Now that Israel was weakened by the yoke of the Philistines, the Ammonites saw their chance to recapture the territory of Gilead. They besieged the city of Jabesh-Gilead. Their king was a cruel, vengeful monarch. As the price of a peace treaty he demanded that the people of Jabesh-Gilead submit to having their right eyes put out, branding them forever with the shame of defeat.

The stone remains of Saul's ancient fortress at Gibeah.

Saul sent messengers from Gibeah throughout the land, asking the tribes to unite at once to help the city of Jabesh-Gilead. The men of Israel responded, and under Saul's capable leadership, Israel attacked the Ammonites, who were besieging the city. Saul's warriors fell upon the Ammonites and sent them fleeing in confusion.

Saul's victory served a double purpose. It vanquished an enemy and, as well, reunited the tribes of Israel. Together, they marched to Gilgal. There, led by Samuel, the people proclaimed Saul their king.

Samuel Is Disappointed

Saul had met Israel's dire need for a courageous and clever military leader; but Samuel was disappointed in the new king. Saul's spiritual values did not always meet the high standards set by the Torah. A rift developed between Samuel the spiritual leader and Saul the warrior king. In his last years Samuel refused even to meet with Saul, and predicted that none of Saul's sons would succeed him on the throne.

Hebrew writing went through several stages before it crystalized into its present form in the 9th or 10th century. Note the early forms of picture writing.

Saul, A Troubled King / ca. 1020–1004 B.C.E.

Search for a New Ruler

Samuel's rejection lay heavily on the mind of King Saul. He became deeply troubled, suffering sleepless nights and days of anguish during which he scarcely spoke to those around him.

Samuel, the aged seer, began to look about secretly for a new king. Inspired by God, his choice fell on David, a shepherd, the youngest son of Jesse of Bethlehem, a farmer of the tribe of Judah. Samuel anointed David in secret and proclaimed him the next king of Israel.

David the Sweet Singer

Saul's advisers had heard about David's outstanding musical talent. Soon after these events they brought the young shepherd to Saul's court to play his harp and sing his songs for the troubled king. In later years, because of his musical gifts, people would call David "the sweet singer of Israel."

The king took a great fancy to the young singer and later gave David his daughter Michal in marriage. David and Jonathan, Saul's eldest son, became very good friends.

David killed the giant Goliath with a stone from a sling. Soldiers with slings fought side-by-side with the archers. A sling consisted of two leather straps and a stone-holder. The sling was whirled until it hummed like a bee. The stone was then released with nearly the speed of a bullet. It hurtled to its target and could cause death or serious injury. This orthostat from the time of David and Solomon shows how the sling was used in battle.

David proved himself as capable in battle as he was with his harp and song. He slew Goliath, a Philistine giant who had terrified the Israelite army. Up and down the land went the stories of David's valiant deeds. "Saul has slain his thousands," the people sang, "but David his ten thousands!" From this, however, David was to learn a bitter lesson: it is always dangerous for a man to become more popular than his king.

Saul Becomes Jealous

Saul became suspicious and jealous of David. The king began to plot to destroy the popular young hero.

Jonathan warns David

Early on Jonathan, the heir to the throne, recognized David's gifts of bravery and leadership. He told David, "You are going to be king over Israel, and I shall be your second."

Musical instruments were common in the ancient Near East. This relief from Ashurbanipal's palace shows a quartet of musicians playing a tambourine, cymbals and a harp.

Jonathan's friendship with David alienated him from his father, King Saul. He secretly warned David when he learned that Saul was planning to kill him. David, accompanied by his most trusted warriors, fled into the mountains of Judah. Saul tracked him down and David realized that he would be safe nowhere in Israel. He was forced to seek refuge in the land of Israel's Philistine enemies. For sixteen months, he and his men were given shelter in the city of Ziklag by King Achish of Gath, who was no doubt secretly elated at this sign of disunity in the land of Israel. Though they were guests of the king, David and his men were closely watched by the Philistines, who did not trust these aliens in their midst.

Saul's Last Battle / ca. 1104 B.C.E.

The Philistine army, encouraged by news of King Saul's troubles, prepared again for all-out attack. Their ranks were greatly reinforced by many fierce mercenaries. The Philistines advanced to the plain of Jezreel. At the foot of Mount Gilboa a bloody battle took place, close to the very spot where Barak and Deborah had once put the Canaanites to rout. There was no glorious victory this time, for the morose and troubled Saul was no longer able to inspire courage and enthusiasm in his warriors. He and his army were overwhelmed by the Philistine onslaught.

The battle at Mount Gilboa was a disastrous defeat for Israel. Many thousands were slain, among them the sons of Saul, including the valiant Jonathan. Saul, dreading the fate of being taken captive, died by his own hand.

The Philistines carried the bodies of Saul and his sons in triumph to their temple at Beth-She'an, where they exhibited them on the temple walls. The loyal men of Jabesh-Gilead, remembering how Saul had once so bravely defended them, removed the bodies in the dark of night to save them from further shame.

David, the "sweet singer," composed a song of mourning, one of the Bible's greatest poems, extolling the courage of the two great warriors and lamenting their fall in battle.

Both Saul and Jonathan!
They were together in life and death.
They were swifter than eagles, stronger than lions.
Now, people of Israel weep for Saul,
Jonathan is slain upon the hills.
How I weep for you, my brother Jonathan;
How much I loved you.

The preferred weapon in the ancient Near East was the bow. This Egyptian painting shows instructors teaching their pupils the art of marksmanship with the bow.

The House of David / ca. 1004–965 B.C.E.

A New Era for Israel

The time that followed the death of Saul was difficult and unhappy for the Israelites. The Philistine tyranny weighed heavily upon them. Taxes of tribute were high, and the presence of Philistine soldiers throughout the land was a constant reminder of Israel's bitter defeat. After Saul's death, civil strife disrupted the tribes, for they could not agree on who was to be Israel's new ruler.

Abner, one of Saul's generals, proclaimed Ishbosheth, the last surviving son of Saul, as king. At the same time, David ruled in Hebron, the capital of Judah. The unfortunate Ishbosheth, who proved to be a weak monarch, was slain by his own men after a reign of only two years. In 1006 B.C.E., after his death, the tribes accepted David as their king.

David, now king over all Israel, scarcely had time to take stock of the new situation before the Philistines, eager to prevent Israel from uniting, marched into the territory of Judah. David hastily assembled all available fighting men. The enemy was forced to fight in the Judean hills, a territory well known to David and his soldiers.

With the assistance of his brilliant general, Joab, David forced battle after battle upon the Philistines. David gave them no peace, attacking ferociously whenever they attempted to rest.

The Philistine city of Gath fell to the Israelites. Soon thereafter the war ended and the battle-weary Philistine army began to dissolve. The Philistine mercenaries, ever ready to follow the winner, came over to the side of Israel and found employment with David's army. The crushing power of the Philistines was broken and their heavy yoke was lifted from the people of Israel.

David playing his harp. Painting is from an Italian prayer book, ca. 1450–1470.

The Israeli archaeologist Abraham Biran has excavated the 4000-year-old site of Tel-Dan. He has found a stone inscription which he believes contains the first-ever mention of the royal House of David.

Jerusalem Is Captured

In the midst of the Judean hills there still remained a fortified city which had resisted every Israelite effort to conquer it since the time of Joshua. This was the city of Jerusalem, the ancient stronghold of the Jebusites.

Joab, David's general, found a chink in Jerusalem's invincible armor. He learned of a secret passage—a natural tunnel that led through the rocky mountains into the center of the city. Joab led his troops through this tunnel, taking the Jebusites by surprise. Thus did Jerusalem become an Israelite city.

Israel, a Growing Nation

The tribes of Israel were now firmly united. Jerusalem became the seat of a central government which dealt with the many issues confronting the nation. David made the city his royal residence, and had the Holy Ark brought there. On festivals throngs of joyous Israelites made the journey to Jerusalem to participate in worship services.

The land of Israel had become a thriving nation, with a splendid capital city of which any people might have been proud and a king to whom even the mightiest monarchs paid homage.

Nathan the Prophet

In addition to Saul's daughter, Michal, David had other wives, as was the custom in the Near East. Among them was Bathsheba, who had been the wife of Uriah, an army captain. David had ordered Uriah into combat, where he was slain. The king then married the captain's beautiful widow. The prophet Nathan rebuked King David, making him aware of the seriousness of his deed. Although David realized that he had done wrong and repented his transgression, Bathsheba remained his favorite wife, and her son, Solomon, became his favorite son.

David Instructs Solomon

When David lay dying, he instructed Solomon as follows: "I am going the way of all earth; be strong and act like a man. Keep the laws of your God, walking in his ways and following his commandments and rules as recorded in the Torah, in order that you succeed in whatever you undertake. Then your descendants will be true in their conduct and will walk before me with all their heart and soul, so that your line on the throne of Israel will never end."

David Chooses Solomon

David found it difficult to decide which of his sons was to succeed him as king. He realized that in order to prevent strife over the succession, he had to announce his choice before he died. Summoning Nathan the prophet, he told him that he had selected the wise Prince Solomon, son of Bathsheba. Solomon was anointed by Zadok, the high priest, and proclaimed king. The rams' horns sounded and the people shouted, "Long live King Solomon!"

King David's work was done. When he died, all Israel mourned the passing of the sweet singer whose many accomplishments had included the composition of the beautiful poems that comprise the biblical Book of Psalms. David died in 965 B.C.E.

The Citadel of David stands on the site over which Herod the Great built his palace in the 1st century B.C.E. At the time of the Jewish revolt against Rome the Citadel of David was one of the main fortifications guarding Jerusalem.

The Byzantine conquerors mistakenly thought that this was David's palace. When the crusaders invaded Palestine, they used the Citadel as a residence, and when they were defeated, Saladin used it as his headquarters. The tall minaret was added in 1655.

34

Solomon, King of Peace / ca. 965–926 B.C.E.

Solomon on the Throne

Solomon took over the reins of government with efficiency. He carefully evaluated Israel's assets, his father's accomplishments, and the possibilities at hand. He completed the fortifications and building projects which David had begun and furthered his trade alliances with other nations.

The friendly alliance between David and King Hiram of Tyre proved advantageous for Solomon, who became a close friend of the Phoenician monarch. Both kings were aware of the importance of Ezion-Geber, Israel's new port on the Red Sea, and both cooperated in enlarging it. Ezion-Geber could open the sea route to India.

With Hiram's assistance, Solomon began building a navy for Israel. Soon Phoenician and Israelite traders were voyaging together, exchanging their wares for the rich offerings of faraway lands. The Israelites exported their most valuable new product, copper from the mines of the Negev. It was the main source of their new wealth.

The Queen of Sheba

Israel's seafarers told many tales about the riches of Arabia and the beauty of its queen. Finally the Queen of Sheba herself journeyed from her far-distant empire in Ophir to visit King Solomon's court. Solomon also forged strategic, commercial, and political ties with his neighbors. In addition to his commercial relations with Hiram of Tyre, he promoted trade with an Egyptian Pharaoh and married one of his daughters. In fact, Solomon made so many matrimonial alliances with foreign royal families that he was said to have 1,000 wives and concubines. These marriages promoted political and commercial treaties.

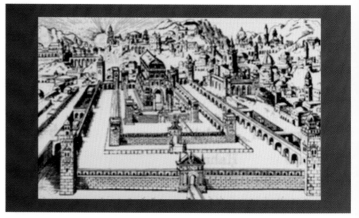

An artist's idea of the Bet Hamikdash, the Temple in Jerusalem. The large area, the Temple Mount, was surrounded by a wall.

This potsherd establishes the existence and wealth of Ophir. It reads: "Gold from Ophir for Beth-Horon." The Book of Kings tells us "They came to Ophir and fetched 400 talents of gold and brought it to King Solomon."

A horned altar from the Solomonic period. Altars of this type were used for sacrifices and incense burning. After the Temple was built, sacrifices were only performed at the Temple by the priests. This altar was discovered at Arad, in the Negev.

Solomon's Temple contained a huge bronze water basin called a "sea", which weighed about 30 tons and held about 10,000 gallons of water. The "sea" contained the water which was used to wash the hands of the priests who took part in the ceremonies.

The Holy Temple

Now Solomon turned to the project which would demand his greatest effort, the one most dear to his heart and the hearts of his people—the building of the Holy Temple (Bet Hamikdash), on Mount Zion. Until now, Israel had worshipped God in the simple sanctuary that housed the Holy Ark. Solomon wanted a more fitting House of God, a magnificent Temple that would be the grandest structure in all Jerusalem, indeed in all the land of Israel.

From his close friend and ally, King Hiram of Tyre, Solomon obtained cedar wood of Lebanon for the Temple. He paid for this precious wood with the produce of Israel—grain and oil, olives and figs—and with copper from the mines of Ezion-Geber.

The Temple was built of stone and precious wood, with great pillars and spacious inner courts, with special places appointed for the various rites of the services. The interior was paneled with cedar wood. Gold, newly brought to the land of Israel from other countries in exchange for copper and olive oil, was lavishly used to make Solomon's Temple a dazzling sight to behold.

Moreover, not one iron tool was used in the construction of the Temple, because of iron's association with violence and war.

Solomon acquired a reputation for great wisdom. Three biblical books, Proverbs, Ecclesiastes (Kohelet), and Song of Songs (Shir Ha Shirim) are attributed to him.

Jerusalem Rejoices

When the Temple was completed, Jerusalem was thronged with jubilant people. Many had come merely to marvel, but many others had come to rejoice and rededicate themselves to their faith.

They also brought wares to trade in the busy markets, they presented their problems and disputes to the judges in the king's court, they left their sacrifices and offerings.

The Romans conquered Jerusalem in 70 C.E. and burned the Temple to the ground. All that remained was the Western Wall, which became a sacred place where Jews prayed. All through the centuries of exile Jews worshipped at the Western Wall. The Wall has become a place for Jews to write prayer and requests to place in the cracks between the stone.

The Seeds of Rebellion

Solomon the Builder

Meantime, a change was taking place in Israel's old way of life. Masses of unskilled laborers were needed for Solomon's many projects and to work in the mines. Great masses of Israelites became poor laborers, while only a few of the people grew rich. The latter were mainly merchants, artisans, designers and builders, chroniclers and officials in the civil service, or officers in the king's army.

The Temple in Jerusalem was only one of Solomon's building projects. He also erected a series of fortified towns, among them Hazor, Gezer, and Beth-Horon. In addition he built dams and wells which allowed cities to withstand enemy sieges. For his chariot troops and cavalry Solomon built large garrison towns and store-cities for munitions and food.

For efficiency Solomon divided the country into twelve taxpaying districts.

Every citizen paid tribute to the king in some way. Taxes were levied on the wealthy for highway construction, building projects, and to pay for the many government officials, soldiers, and royal servants. The poor who had no money to pay their taxes had to contribute their services to the king as laborers or soldiers. Samuel's warning, which had gone unheeded by the people of Israel so long ago, now seemed to echo across the years. The people had chosen to be ruled by a king, and they were paying a heavy price, both in property and in freedom.

Some of the lands which David had conquered became restless under Solomon's rule. They felt confident that Solomon, unlike his father, would not march against them if they revolted. One by one, the outlying territories began to break away.

One section of the ruins of King Solomon's stables at Meggido.

A reconstruction of the stables.

Discontent Grows

As Solomon's reign proceeded, the northern tribes became discontented, chafing under their heavy burden of taxes and forced labor. They felt that they were not benefiting from Solomon's policies. Trouble exploded when Jeroboam, the official in charge of labor and building projects for the district of Joseph, plotted rebellion.

Solomon, wise and wealthy, was reaping a golden harvest, but the seeds of discontent were sprouting uncomfortably close to the throne. Many of his nobles disapproved of the king's tolerance toward foreign priests and his foreign wives, who prayed to their own idols under Solomon's roof.

A reconstruction of Solomon's Temple.

Throughout the land many who longed for the simpler ways of days gone by. As far as they were concerned, Solomon valued wealth and pomp far too highly, at a price the Israelites were reluctant to pay.

King Solomon Dies / ca. 926 B.C.E.

Solomon died after a reign of 40 years. The combined reigns of David and Solomon covered a span of 80 years, during which Israel grew into an important, wealthy nation.

Rehoboam the Successor

In 928 B.C.E., Rehoboam, the son whom Solomon had named as his successor, was proclaimed king. Yet the throne which Solomon's son ascended was resting on shaky foundations.

Rehoboam lacked the great ability of his father and grandfather, but he was a prince of the House of David and the tribe of Judah followed him loyally. The northern tribes warned Rehoboam that they would not be his loyal subjects unless he met their demands.

The elders of the northern tribes did not go to Jerusalem to pay homage to the new king; instead, they asked Rehoboam to come to an assembly at Shechem in the territory of Ephraim.

Rehoboam Refuses Concessions

When the northern leaders asked the young king to give them assurance that he would lighten their taxes and ease their burdens, Rehoboam kept them waiting three days for his answer. Solomon's old advisors, experienced in the ways of government, strongly urged Rehoboam to grant the request, pointing out that the loyalty of the northern tribes was an important asset to the kingdom. Rehoboam refused to make any concessions. Instead, he arrogantly informed the northern tribes that he would demand even higher taxes and more labor services than his father had required.

The Kingdom Is Divided / ca. 926 B.C.E.

Rehoboam the Arrogant / ca. 926–910 B.C.E.

Angered and offended by Rehoboam's arrogance, the northern tribes rose up in revolt. Had Rehoboam listened to the advice of wiser heads, it is possible that the united kingdom could have been saved. But he insolently rejected the demands.

When the people of Shechem petitioned him for relief, he replied, "My father, Solomon, punished you with a whip, but I will punish you with scorpions." Only the tribes of Judah and Benjamin remained loyal to the young monarch. The other ten tribes chose a new leader—Jeroboam, the veteran rebel from the northern tribe of Ephraim. Jeroboam had been in exile in Egypt, where he had gained the support of Pharaoh Shishak. As the ambitious head of a new dynasty, Shishak was delighted at the prospect of disunity in Israel and encouraged Jeroboam to return home as soon as he learned of Solomon's death.

Taking advantage of the crisis at Shechem, Jeroboam raised the standard of revolt against Rehoboam. The situation

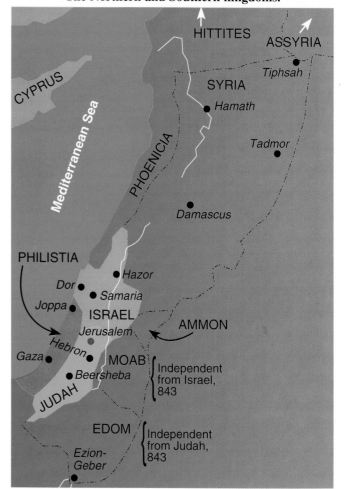

ISRAEL AND JUDAH
The Northern and Southern kingdoms.

became so threatening that Rehoboam and his advisors fled back to Jerusalem.

Two Kingdoms: Israel and Judah / ca. 926 B.C.E.

As a result of the fateful assembly at Shechem, the flourishing kingdom of David and Solomon was divided into two smaller states, the northern kingdom of Israel, under Jeroboam, and the southern kingdom of Judah, under Rehoboam.

A bronze statue from Samaria. The Canaanites were idol-worshippers, and this bull is thought to have been one of their gods.

KINGS BEFORE DIVISION OF KINGDOM

1020–1004 B.C.E.	SAUL	
1004–965 B.C.E.	DAVID	THE NORTHERN
965–928 B.C.E.	SOLOMON	KINGDOM OF ISRAEL

All dates are approximate

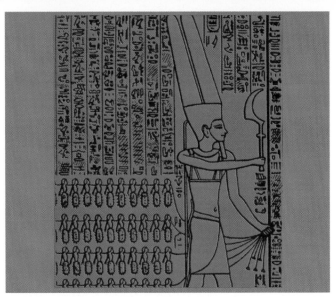

Pharaoh Shishak immortalized his victory over King Rehoboam in a relief on the wall of the great temple in Karnak. In his hands can be seen the ropes by which he leads the captives from the conquered cities of Judah. Each captive represents a different city.

Throughout the reigns of Rehoboam and Jeroboam, there was war between Israel and Judah. Each kingdom fortified its frontier. Judah reinforced many of its fortresses, but despite this, much of its power had been lost and a great deal of its influence weakened. The powerful empire created by David and Solomon was no more, and many former allies abandoned the House of David.

Egypt Attacks Israel / ca. 922 B.C.E.
Judah suffered another great blow when Shishak of Egypt attacked in the fifth year of Rehoboam's reign. The advance of Shishak's army was swift and unexpected. One after another Judah's fortresses fell, and Jerusalem was taken without a struggle. Shishak spared the Holy City the horror of destruction but ransacked Judah's treasury and marched back to Egypt laden with booty. Among the prizes were many of the golden vessels from the Temple and the famous golden shields which Solomon's guards had carried so proudly. Judah was left impoverished.

Jeroboam Abandons Jerusalem
The people of the northern kingdom of Israel still looked to Jerusalem as their sacred city. On festival days they journeyed there to join the people of Judah in prayers, sacrifices, and holiday processions. Jeroboam, ambitious to be recognized as head of a new royal line entirely separate from Judah, looked with misgivings upon the devotion of his subjects to the Temple. He feared that this bond between the two kingdoms would eventually serve to unite them again.

Idol Worship in Israel
Jeroboam had altars and shrines erected in Bethel and Dan to entice his people to offer prayers and sacrifices in their own land rather than in Jerusalem. In open violation of the Ten Commandments he placed images of golden calves in the shrines, proclaiming that they were representations of the God of Israel.

Jeroboam's purpose in introducing idol worship was twofold. He hoped that it would strengthen his power over his own people and serve further to cement his bond with Egypt.

Thoughtful and faithful Israelites were bitterly disappointed in their king and fervently hoped for a time when things would change. Weakened as they were, there was little to do now but bide their time.

Prophetic Voices

The Prophets

Although it seemed that this dark night of disunity would spell the final decline for Israel, faint signs of a new dawn began to appear on the horizon. Strong new voices were heard among the people of Israel and Judah—often in humble places, in caves and on mountainsides, by the roadside or at the city gates. These were the voices of the prophets, explaining how the ways of man should serve the ways of God.

The prophets went from place to place, caring for neither wealth nor physical comfort. Often they traveled in groups, singing and praying together to the accompaniment of their own music. Wherever the prophets went, the people gathered.

The Assyrian Threat

During these unhappy years, a great new power began to assert itself in Mesopotamia. This was the kingdom of Assyria, whose powerful armies were marching out to conquer all the nations from the Mediterranean to the Euphrates, from Egypt to Lebanon. The prophets of Israel warned the people about the threat posed by this new enemy, a cruel master that showed little mercy to those it conquered, and would suppress the worship of the one God.

The Split Between Judah and Israel

The conflict between Judah and Israel resulted in a stalemate. Israel, the northern kingdom, was larger in both land and population. It was also wealthier and more favorably situated on the busy caravan routes connecting Asia and Egypt. Judah was more compact and far less involved in regional contacts and conflicts. Both kingdoms, however, were at the mercy of their neighbors, Egypt, Aram, and Syria, which managed to preserve a power balance between the two.

The Splendor Is Gone

Much of the outer splendor of Jerusalem was gone, but its marketplaces were still crowded and busy. Here farmers and shepherds exchanged livestock, grain, olive oil, and honey for textiles and leather, vessels and tools, spices and imported goods of every kind. The people of Judah were proud of their famous capital, high in the mountains, with its fortifications and palaces, its markets and fine buildings. They were proud, too, that they were still ruled by the same dynasty which had given them such great kings as David and Solomon. Until the very end, Judah was ruled by an uninterrupted line of kings of the House of David.

Idol Worship

The rulers of the northern kingdom of Israel encouraged the people to worship the idols at the shrines established by Jeroboam. The new kingdom was a constant battleground between two ways of

Acient wall drawings of two Assyrians court officials. These drawings were found in the ruins of a palace on the banks of the Euphrates River.

to the south and, most important, to Phoenicia in the north.

Omri reverted to the tradition of King Solomon and traded with the Phoenicians. He fortified Israel and brought peace and prosperity to the land. For the first time since its beginning, the northern kingdom was secure among its neighbors and free of bloodshed. But, although he was shrewd in battle and wise in the ways of commerce, Omri was not sensitive to the people's spiritual needs and ideals, and as the Bible says, he "did evil in the eyes of God."

Ahab and Jezebel / ca. 871–852 B.C.E.

When Omri died, Ahab became king. Intent on cementing his pact with Phoenicia, Ahab married a Phoenician princess, Jezebel. She brought her idols and priests to her new home in Samaria. Strongly influenced by Jezebel, his vain and haughty wife, Ahab set up shrines to Baal, the most popular Phoenician god.

The famous Moabite Stone, discovered by archaeologists in 1868, records how Moab was enslaved by the House of Omri and made to pay tribute.

life: the way of the Torah and the God of Israel against the way of idol worship and paganism. Many people from Israel still made pilgrimages to the Temple in Jerusalem.

Because it never developed a stable succession, the northern kingdom was ruled by nine separate dynasties. It had five different kings within just a few years of the death of Jeroboam.

The Reign of Omri / ca. 871 B.C.E.

Omri, an able general, established order in Israel. He defeated the Moabites and made them Israel's vassals. He built a beautiful new capital, Samaria. It became an important city, well fortified and strategically located in the central hills of Ephraim. From Samaria new trade routes developed

Jezebel, with the priests of Baal, set about teaching the Phoenician way of life to the people of Israel, persecuting anyone who defied her. Many of the prophets were killed at her command. Many others escaped, however, for the people protected them.

Bronze statue of an idol excavated from the ancient city of Megiddo.

Elijah and Elisha

Elijah Fights for Justice / ca. 869–849 B.C.E.

Not many people had the courage to criticize Ahab and Jezebel openly. There was one, however, who would not be silenced. This was the prophet Elijah. Boldly and passionately Elijah spoke out for the poor, who according to the laws of Israel were to be afforded protection from oppression and unjust taxes.

Elijah spoke out fearlessly against the priests of Baal. He fought their influence, upholding and defending the ancient traditions and faith of the people of Israel.

Elijah's most famous feat took place on the slopes of Mount Carmel. In order to prove that Baal was a false god, he challenged the Phoenician priests to a contest. While the assembled people watched, he and

A seal which belonged to an official of King Ahaz, King of Judah. It reads, "Ushana, servant of Ahaz."

they prepared to offer sacrifices on wood saturated with water. When the priests urged Baal to set the wood afire, nothing happened. When Elijah asked God to do the same, the thoroughly soaked wood burst into flames.

Wherever he journeyed, Elijah comforted the poor, healed the sick, and encouraged people to serve God. In many places he destroyed the shrines of Baal. From all sides, Elijah heard shocking stories about King Ahab's cruelty.

Naboth's Vineyard

A man named Naboth owned a beautiful vineyard near Ahab's palace. Despite the king's threats, Naboth had refused to sell the vineyard, for it had been in his family for generations. The ruthless Jezebel arranged to have Naboth falsely accused of sacrilege and treason. Naboth suffered the punishment customarily inflicted on those who committed this crime—he was stoned to death.

Elijah was outraged. He went to see Ahab, prophesying the destruction of the House of Omri as a dynasty which had become unfit to rule. Struck with remorse, Ahab mourned, fasted, and asked God's forgiveness. Unfortunately, his repentance and good intentions were no match for the influence of Queen Jezebel.

Elijah in Jewish Tradition

Elijah was greatly loved by the people of Israel. Stories of his bravery, his compassion, his helpfulness to the poor and sick, were told through the length and breadth of the land. In time, he was to become a symbol of the spirit of redemption.

According to the biblical story, Elijah and his disciple Elisha were walking along the banks of the Jordan River when a fiery chariot suddenly descended next to them. Elijah threw his prophetic mantle to Elisha

The stone tower of Jezebel in Jezreel.

and stepped into the chariot, which flew upward and vanished from sight. Elisha picked up the mantle and assumed the leadership of the crusade against idolatry.

Jewish tradition believes that Elijah did not die, but will one day appear to announce the coming of the Messiah. Each year on Passover, on Seder night, when Jews celebrate their deliverance from Egypt, they remember Elijah, the symbol and spirit of freedom.

Elijah Calls Elisha to Prophecy

Elisha was Elijah's disciple. The Bible tells how Elijah recruited him. While passing through the Jordan Valley, Elijah saw Elisha plowing a field with a team of oxen. From a distance, he sensed the extraordinary power in the strong, sweat-soaked farmer. Without hesitation, Elijah removed his mantle and flung it around the young man's shoulders. This was an ancient symbolic call to prophetic service which Elisha eagerly accepted.

Both prophets devoted themselves to the crusade against idolatry, but there was a definite difference between them. Elijah was stern and solitary, while Elisha was gentle and was often found in the company of his disciples.

Elisha performed miracles and was active in the political and military life of Israel. When the Israelite army attacked Moab, he saved the day by finding water for the troops. Elisha also played a major role in the events leading to the seizure of power by Jehu. Determined to dethrone the idol-worshipping King Jehoram, Elisha sent one of his disciples to anoint Jehu, thus inducing him to revolt.

Elisha's fame as a miracle worker was so great that legend attributed power to him even after his death. One day, mourners at a funeral were attacked by Moabite

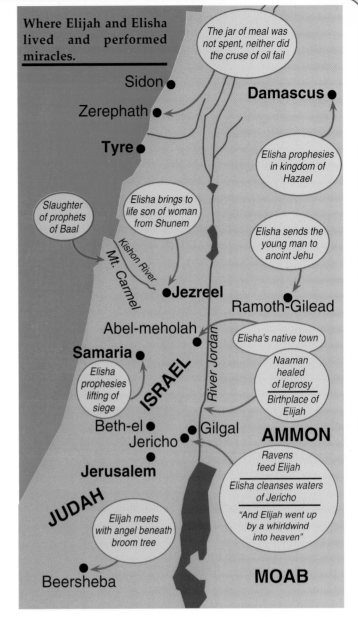

Where Elijah and Elisha lived and performed miracles.

- The jar of meal was not spent, neither did the cruse of oil fail
- Sidon
- Zerephath
- Damascus
- Tyre
- Elisha prophesies in kingdom of Hazael
- Slaughter of prophets of Baal
- Elisha brings to life son of woman from Shunem
- Elisha sends the young man to anoint Jehu
- Kishon River
- Mt. Carmel
- Jezreel
- Ramoth-Gilead
- Abel-meholah
- River Jordan
- Elisha's native town
- Samaria
- ISRAEL
- Elisha prophesies lifting of siege
- Naaman healed of leprosy
- Birthplace of Elijah
- Beth-el
- Jericho
- Gilgal
- AMMON
- Jerusalem
- Ravens feed Elijah
- Elisha cleanses waters of Jericho
- "And Elijah went up by a whirldwind into heaven"
- JUDAH
- Elijah meets with angel beneath broom tree
- Beersheba
- MOAB

bandits. The frightened mourners threw the corpse into the nearby tomb of Elisha and fled. On contacting the prophet's bones, the corpse came to life and walked away.

A 12th century miniature shows ravens bringing food to prophet Elijah.

The House of Omri

Ahab's Alliances

King Ahab was successful in his military campaigns and in establishing friendly relations with Israel's neighbors. Like all the rulers of the Middle East, he kept a wary eye on the growing power of Assyria; he was well aware that its armies were advancing closer and closer to his country. Realizing the importance of obtaining allies against these powerful conquerors, Ahab gave his daughter Athaliah in marriage to Jehoram, crown prince of Judah, thus strengthening Israel's bond with that country. When Ahab became involved in a war with Aram, Judah helped him to win the victory.

Ahab's pacts with Judah, Aram, Phoenicia, and Moab were well-timed, for the Assyrian army commanded by King Shalmaneser III was drawing nearer. Ahab and his allies met the Assyrians in battle at Carchemish. The coalition resisted valiantly, and in the end Shalmaneser's host departed.

Ahab was succeeded by his son Ahaziah, but he soon fell ill and died. He was followed by his brother Joram, the last king of the House of Omri.

An ivory found at Arslan-Tash in Syria shows a woman, possibly the goddess Astarte, framed in a window. It is thought to be part of the booty taken from Aram-Damascus by the Assyrians in the 8th century B.C.E.

The End of the House of Omri / ca. 845 B.C.E.

With the support of the prophet Elisha, Jehu, one of the king's officers, led a revolt against Jehoram. Elisha was confident that Jehu, once he became king, would abolish idol worship and govern in accordance with the Torah. Jehu's revolt was successful but bloody. Among the victims was Queen Jezebel, and with her all the members of the House of Omri. Jehu now ascended the throne.

Athaliah Becomes Queen / ca. 851 B.C.E.

Jehu's revolt in Israel had grave consequences for Judah. King Ahaziah of Judah was killed in ambush on his journey home from Samaria, where he had been visiting his cousins of the House of Omri. Ahaziah's mother, the ambitious Queen Athaliah, was a true daughter of Jezebel and Ahab. When Athaliah learned of her son's death, she saw her chance to become ruler of Judah. She had all the princes of the House of David killed, no matter how closely they were related to her; ascending the throne, she proved to be a ruthless and tyrannical ruler.

Unknown to Athaliah, one prince had escaped her henchmen: Joash, her grandson. The child had been saved by his uncle Jehoiada, the high priest, who for seven years kept him hidden.

When the time seemed ripe for revolt, Jehoiada brought the young prince before the elders of Judah and Joash was anointed king. This brought Athaliah's tyrannical reign to an end, and the House of David was established in Judah once more.

Jehu / ca. 845–818 B.C.E.

Jehu, who had overthrown Jehoram to become king of Israel, was the first ruler of the northern kingdom to forbid idol worship. At last the people could worship God openly. However, Jehu was not successful in foreign relations. To ward off an invasion by Damascus, he sent tribute to King Shalmaneser of Assyria and asked for his protection. Despite this, Damascus marched against Israel. Jehu was defeated, and Israel became a tribute-paying vassal of Damascus.

War with Damascus

In the days of Jehoahaz, the son of Jehu, the kingdom of Israel suffered severely under the yoke of the Arameans of Damascus and struggled for many years to free itself.

Jehoash / ca. 802–787 B.C.E.

King Jehoash, the son of Jehoahaz, fought Aram three times and finally was victorious. Now it was the Arameans of Damascus who paid tribute to Israel.

Joash reigned for 40 years. During the first part of his reign he accepted the advice of the high priest Jehoiada, but when Jehoiada died, Joash permitted and fostered the worship of idols. Joash was intensely disliked for his religious laxity and military failures. He was slain in his bed by his servants and was succeeded by his son Amaziah.

The black obelisk was set up by Shalmaneser III in his palace at Nimrod. It is inscribed with the story of his battles.

One of the panels on the obelisk shows King Jehu of Israel surrendering to the Assyrian king. Jehu is on his knees, bowing before the victorious Shalmaneser.

Relief on the black obelisk set up by Shalmaneser III shows Israelites bringing tribute to Shalmaneser. The tribute consists of gold, silver, and lead bars.

A Time of Prosperity

A time of prosperity now began for Israel. Samaria, its capital, was a flourishing city. The reign of Jeroboam II, son of Jehoash, saw foreign merchants coming once more to Israel's markets. New trade pacts were signed with the Phoenicians of Tyre.

Unfortunately, Israel's new prosperity was limited to the nobles and the merchants, who failed to remember that the poor were their brothers. Workers were underpaid and rich farmers dealt unfairly with their help. The builders exploited the masons. Workers and small farmers paid high taxes and lived in huts, while the rich lived in luxury.

Jeroboam II (784–748 B.C.E.), like other rulers before him, restored Israel's material wealth and power but had no understanding of people's inner needs. He neglected the laws of the Torah and encouraged his people to adopt the idol-worshiping ways of Damascus and Tyre. The kingdom of Jeroboam appeared strong and powerful, but inwardly it was weak and unjust.

Amos Speaks for Justice / ca. 780–760 B.C.E.

Now another strong voice arose in the land, crying out against the oppressors who were forcing the greater part of the people to endure poverty and injustice. Amos, a shepherd from Tekoa, spoke openly in the streets of Samaria, declaring that the sacrifices made by the rich on the altar at Bethel were meaningless as long as the donors did not act justly.

Amos possessed great knowledge of the political problems of the day. He warned that all the wealth of Samaria would be useless against the Assyrian threat unless the kingdom of Israel was united and strong. This would only come about, he declared, if the nation kept the laws of the Torah.

Israel's wealthy class was annoyed by the prophet. They forced Amos to leave Samaria, but he continued to speak out fearlessly, telling the rich that God would be more pleased by acts of justice than by costly offerings.

Hosea the Prophet

Soon another, younger prophet began to speak in Israel. This was Hosea, who was to witness not only the prosperity of Israel under Jeroboam II, but also a time of

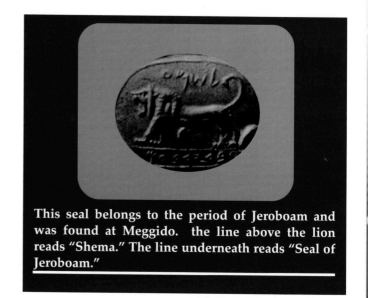

This seal belongs to the period of Jeroboam and was found at Meggido. the line above the lion reads "Shema." The line underneath reads "Seal of Jeroboam."

unhappy changes. The death of Jeroboam was followed by a quick succession of kings and a time of greed, murder, and decay which hastened the destruction of the kingdom.

Hosea's Warnings / ca. 760–755 B.C.E.

Like Amos, Hosea possessed both spiritual and political vision. He foresaw Assyria's invasion of Israel and warned the people to arm themselves morally against the coming time of danger.

Assyria the Conqueror

Assyria had conquered all of Babylonia, and its mighty armies were drawing ever closer. In the light of this threat, Israel, Judah, Aram, and Tyre drew closer to one another. They were in a strategically difficult position, for they stood on the road from Mesopotamia to the Nile Valley. Assyria, they knew, would inevitably attack Egypt, its strongest rival, and before it could do so would have to overrun them. Egypt attempted to persuade the smaller nations to join in an anti-Assyrian alliance. King Menachem of Israel faced with a tough decision: which of the two giants would be a better ally, or, rather, which would be the less ruthless overlord? He made his choice—and sent his tribute to Assyria.

This drawing of the ruthless Assyrian king Tiglath Pileser III, was discovered in the ruins of a palace on the banks of the Euphrates River. The king subjugated the people of Israel and Judah. In his annals the king lists the payments of tribute by King Menachem of Israel and King Ahaz of Judah.

Tiglath-Pileser III / ca. 734 B.C.E.

Meanwhile, another revolt took place in Israel. Menachem's son, Pekahiah, perished in the rebellion, and Pekah, one of the soldiers who had led the uprising, became king. Pekah joined the alliance of small nations along the Mediterranean coast that planned to resist Assyria. Israel was now allied with Edom, the Philistine city-states, Phoenicia, and the Arameans in a desperate effort to ward off Assyria.

A new king named Pul now sat on the Assyrian throne. Better known as Tiglath-Pileser III, he was a soldier who had risen from the ranks. He and his sons were cruel rulers, dedicated only to conquest.

King Ahaz of Judah / ca. 742–725 B.C.E.

Pekah invited King Ahaz of Judah, who was already a vassal of Assyria, to join the coalition. Ahaz firmly refused, for he did not believe Assyria could be defeated. He chose to stay out of the war, but the allies, bent on winning his support, marched against Jerusalem to force him to change his mind. Ahaz asked for Assyria's help in ridding Judah of the invaders.

At this dark moment, Israel again was torn by revolt. King Hoshea (733–724 B.C.E.), a rebel who had taken Pekah's throne, ruled over the remnant of what had once been the northern kingdom. He hoped for an opportunity to shake off the Assyrian yoke and win back Israel's northern lands. When Tiglath-Pileser died, Hoshea made an alliance with Egypt and refused to pay further tribute to Assyria.

Hoshea survived this time, but the allies who attempted to withstand Assyria fared badly. The Assyrians had already begun their march to Egypt. The people of Israel were filled with forebodings about the future.

Israel Falls / ca. 721 B.C.E.

The Reign of Shalmaneser V / ca. 727–722 B.C.E.

Shalmaneser V, the new Assyrian king, would tolerate no rebellion. He invaded Israel at once and laid siege to Samaria, the capital. Samaria had been wisely planned and well-fortified by Omri, however, and for three years its valiant defenders withstood the invaders. Shalmaneser died during the siege, but his successor, Sargon II, continued the campaign. Samaria finally fell to Sargon in the first year of his reign (721 B.C.E.).

As always, Assyria dealt ruthlessly with the conquered nation. Israel's leaders and best-educated, most skilled people were deported. All signs of opposition were suppressed. The region that had once been the proudly independent kingdom of Israel was made part of the Assyrian province of Syria.

The Ten Lost Tribes

Sargon deported 27,290 Israelites to distant countries far from their homeland. Scattered in strange lands and broken in spirit, the conquered people posed no threat of revolt to their captors and eventually lost their religious identity. Ever since they have been referred to as the Ten Lost Tribes.

To repopulate the areas left desolate by the war and the deportations, people from other lands conquered by the Assyrians were moved to Israel. The foreigners brought their own customs and religions with them. As they mingled with the surviving Israelites, a new people known as the Samaritans eventually emerged.

The northern kingdom of Israel was no more; its glory had vanished, its people were gone. Those few who had escaped to Judah told tales of suffering and defeat.

A stone tablet with the victory inscription of Sargon II. " I besieged Samaria and carried off 27,290 of its people as booty."

The kings of Israel in order of succession. The list starts with Jeroboam in 937 B.C.E. and ends with the destruction of Samaria in 722 B.C.E.

937–722 BCE

1. JEROBOAM
2. NADAB
3. BAASA (BAASHA)
4. ELAH
5. ZIMRI
6. OMRI
7. AHAB
8. AHAZIAH
9. JEHORAM (JORAM)
10. JEHU
11. JEHOAZ
12. JEHOHASH
13. JEROBOAM II
14. ZECHARIAH
15. SHALLUM
16. MENAHEM
17. PEKAHIAH
18. PEKAH
19. HOSHEA

The Assyrians destroy Samaria and lead the Ten Tribes into captivity.

They now realized that the warnings of Hosea and Amos had indeed been prophetic.

Religion played a key role in Judea and in Israel. Despite its defeats, Judah remained loyal to the God of Abraham, Isaac, and Jacob.

In what had been the northern kingdom, however, the worship of Baal and other gods was prevalent. The remaining Israelite inhabitants were demoralized; they had no religious shield to protect them from their idol-worshipping neighbors, the foreign settlers brought in by the Assyrians. Before long they blended with the pagan population and disappeared as a nation.

After a long and bloody battle, Lachish was captured by the Babylonians. To instill fear, the Judean captives were impaled on stakes and hung on the walls. This event was recorded on a relief in Shalmaneser IV's palace at Nineveh.

THE END OF THE KINGDOM OF ISRAEL

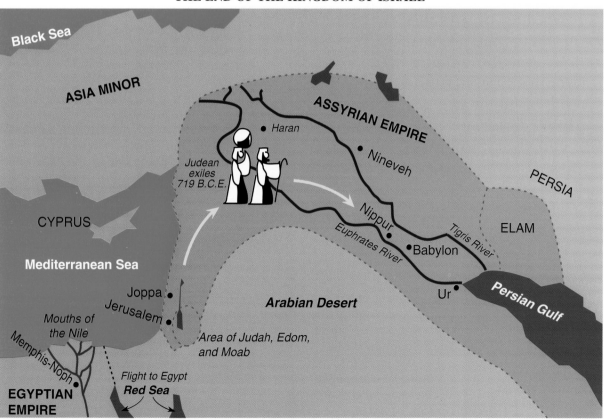

The annals of Sargon II, king of Assyria, state, "I besieged and conquered Samaria. I led away 27,290 of its inhabitants as captives."

Isaiah, Statesman and Prophet

In contrast to turbulent Israel, the little kingdom of Judah lived rather peacefully for many years. Since it was remote from the main caravan routes, it did not seek important trade and military pacts and most of its kings tried to avoid war. The splendor of Solomon's days was gone, but the real glory still remained—the Temple on Mount Zion in Jerusalem. Here the people of Judah brought their offerings and celebrated their festivals.

When King Ahaz (742–725 B.C.E.) faced the difficult choice between appeasing Assyria and joining the other small nations in an anti-Assyrian alliance, he turned for advice to a man of great brilliance and wisdom. This was the prophet Isaiah, who had counseled the royal family for three generations. Isaiah was well-educated, born into a noble family. Drawing on his wide knowledge of Judah's political problems, he advised Ahaz not to join the alliance, for he was positive that the allies would be no match for the mighty Assyrian war machine. Ahaz followed Isaiah's advice.

Ahaz Appeases Assyria

Soon after this came the news that the alliance had been defeated. All Judah mourned the destruction of Israel and the plight of the helpless thousands lost in captivity in far-off Assyria. Frightened lest Judah share the same fate, Ahaz tried in every way to win the favor of the Assyrians. He began to follow the Assyrian way of life and worship, even installing idols in the Temple. Isaiah, who had advised neutrality, not submission, was bitterly disappointed and criticized Ahaz severely. He foresaw that the king's policy would bring nothing but disaster to Judah.

The Isaiah Scroll, one of the scrolls discovered in a cave in the Dead Sea area. This is one of the oldest parts of the Bible ever found.

The grave of King Uzziah is marked by this engraved stone tablet. The inscription reads:
To this place (lit. hither) were brought the bones of Uzziah King of Judah. Do not open!

Stone encased in its original copper setting. On the face is carved the figure of a ram. Above the ram is the name of the owner, Jonathan. This name was borne by a Judean king. Uzziah's son was named Jonathan.

Prophets of Peace

Foreseeing the destruction of Judah, Isaiah wrote prophecies of great comfort and compassion during these dark days. Inspired by visions of hope and longing for the happiness of all humankind, the prophet wrote of the day when all peoples would live together in harmony, serving the one God—the God of peace.

Today, high on a marble wall opposite the United Nations Building in New York City, are engraved the words of Isaiah's ancient prophecy of peace, for all the peoples of the world to read and ponder:

They shall beat their swords into plowshares, and their spears into pruning hooks. Nation shall not lift up sword against nation, neither shall they learn war any more (Isaiah 2:4).

The prophet Isaiah and his younger contemporary Micah shared the same ideals of faith and peace. Their voices were heard throughout Judah, and while the people often seemed indifferent, the inspiring words of these two great prophets left a deep impression.

This Khorsabad painting shows Sargon and an officer before an Assyrian god.

The marble wall opposite the United Nations Building.

Micah the Prophet

Another prophet who spoke in those days was Micah, a young man of humble birth from the small village of Moresheth-Gath in the Judean hills. Micah grieved for Samaria and wept for the sufferings of the people of Israel. He warned the people of Judah not to forsake the Torah. As Amos had done before him. Micah reminded the people that God wanted more of them than sacrificial offerings.

"What does God require of thee," cried Micah, "save to do justice and to love mercy and to walk humbly with thy God!"

This is the opening page to the Book of Isaiah, from a Bible copied in Portugal, in the 15th century.

King Hezekiah Rebels

Hezekiah Rules / ca. 725–697 B.C.E.

Ahaz was succeeded by his son Hezekiah. Heeding Isaiah's warnings, Hezekiah rid Judah of the idols his father had installed and strengthened the nation by upholding its laws and traditions.

Unrest was breaking out among the countries which had been conquered by the Assyrians. Hezekiah joined the general spirit of revolt and refused to pay further tribute to Assyria. Egyptian envoys came to Jerusalem and secret conferences were held. Envoys from the Babylonian king in far-off Mesopotamia also came to seek Hezekiah's aid against the hated Assyrian giant. Egypt and Babylonia had already formed an alliance.

Quietly and efficiently, Hezekiah prepared Judah for revolt. He devised a major engineering project to increase the city's water supply. The waters of the river Gihon were diverted into a reservoir, called the

The Hebrew inscription found in the tunnel of Siloam. "The tunnel (is completed). And this is the story of the boring through: While yet they plied the pick, each toward his fellow, and while yet there were three cubits to be bored through, there was heard the voice of one calling to another, for there was a crevice in the rock on the right hand. And on the day of the boring through, the stone-cutters struck, each to meet his fellow, pick upon pick; and the waters flowed from the source to the pool for a thousand and two hundred cubits, and a hundred cubits was the height of the rock above the heads of the stone-cutters."

Pool of Siloam, and an underground tunnel was constructed to bring the water into the city.

Sennacherib Invades Judah / ca. 701 B.C.E.

When Sargon died, the rebellious allies thought the time had come to strike against Assyria. However, Sargon's successor, Sennacherib, learned that rebellion was brewing, and went forth with a large army to crush it. Hezekiah's preparations had been made just in time, for Sennacherib invaded Judah, storming its fortresses and smashing great holes in their walls with his battering rams.

Sennacherib laid siege to Jerusalem. Guided by Hezekiah and the prophet Isaiah, the people of the city bore up bravely, but as the siege wore on, food became so scarce that surrender seemed inevitable.

Then an unexpected ally came to the beleaguered city's rescue. Plague, that dread disease of ancient times, providentially struck

Underground tunnel leading to the pool of Siloam.

the Assyrian camp. Thousands of Assyrian soldiers perished in the epidemic and were buried in hastily-dug mass graves.

The prophet Isaiah mourned for the ravaged land of Judah. Towns and cities were burned or lay in ruin. Yet, even in the midst of the ruins there were prayers of thanksgiving, for the people had survived the Assyrian onslaught.

Assyria Rules

Sennacherib returned to Nineveh, where all his energies were now required to defend his empire. Uprisings had broken out close to his capital, in Mesopotamia itself. Sennacherib finally suffered the same fate as his father. In 681 B.C.E. he was assassinated. He was succeeded by his son Esarhaddon, who had to fight almost continuously to maintain his power. The great Assyrian Empire, seemingly about to crumble, was still a force to be reckoned with.

When Hezekiah died, his son Manasseh submitted completely to Assyrian rule, even reinstating idol worship to appease the foreign overlords.

Manasseh, an Obedient Servant / ca. 696–642 B.C.E.

The aging Isaiah, whose voice had been heard for so many years, now foresaw Judah's destruction and fall, and again warned of the consequences of abandoning the Torah's ancient laws. But the words of the old man went unheeded.

Manasseh was an obedient Assyrian vassal. The country was impoverished by the high taxes he collected for his Assyrian masters. Foreign idols stood in the Temple of God, and corruption reigned among the nobles of Judah, even reaching into the lives of the Levites and priests. After Isaiah

died, and his voice was no longer a comforting and inspiring force, many Judeans turned to the Assyrian idols.

Despite Manasseh's submissiveness, Assyrian officials began to doubt his loyalty. They summoned him to Nineveh to punish him. In exile he suffered great indignities. When he returned to Jerusalem he had changed completely. His deep remorse is shown by a prayer he composed around this time, which is preserved among the postbiblical writings known as the Apocrypha:

You (before) whom all things fear and tremble;
(especially) before your power.
Because your awesome magnificence
cannot be endured;
none can endure or stand before
your anger and your fury against sinners!
But unending and immeasurable
are your promised mercies;
Because you are God,
long-suffering, merciful, and greatly compassionate;
and you feel sorry over the evils of men.

At the end of his long reign, Manasseh was succeeded by his son Amon (642–640 B.C.E.). This unfortunate king was soon assassinated by a group of palace officials. The plotters were quickly captured and executed, and Amon's son Josiah was placed on the throne.

Victory monument of King Esarhaddon. He is leading two captive kings on a leash attached to hooks which pass through their lips.

54

Decline of Assyria

More and more new threats of revolt plagued the successors of Ashurbanipal. While Assyria was busy keeping its many rebellious vassals in check, the empire was suddenly invaded by the Scythians, a people from the Black Sea region. Wild and fearless riders, they came on horseback, plundering and looting wherever they went. Hordes of Scythian horsemen raced through Assyria's territories, and throughout the entire Fertile Crescent.

Josiah the Reformer / ca. 639–609 B.C.E.
While the Scythian hordes swept through ancient empires, a new king had come to the throne of Judah. Josiah, the son of Amon, was a very different man from his father. Josiah heeded the words of the prophet Zephaniah, who had criticized the corruption that prevailed in Judah in the days of Amon. The new king rid the land of idols and corrupt officials, and returned to the laws of Israel and the worship of one God. Josiah had all the idols destroyed and the Temple thoroughly cleansed.

A Great Discovery
During the process of cleansing the Temple, a great discovery was made. A scroll was found which had lain forgotten and lost for generations. When examined the scroll was found to be the Book of Deuteronomy, the last of the Five Books of Moses. It summarized and explained the Ten Commandments and the laws of Israel. Hilkiah, the high priest, and Huldah, a prophetess, encouraged the king to study this long-lost book and read it aloud to the people of Judah. Standing before a large assembly, Josiah read from the Book of Deuteronomy, as the people, young and old, stood listening in awe to the ancient words.

All over Judah priests assembled the people and read to them from the book. The people became familiar with their history and traditions. Most important of all, the Book of Deuteronomy taught the people the meaning of their laws. Strengthened by this new knowledge, the people of Judah regained faith and dignity.

Such was the state of Judah when Assyria was dealt its final blow. Two prophets, Nahum and Zephaniah, had prophesied that the destruction of Assyria was at hand. Josiah had heard and believed these prophecies. Now they came true. After the death of Ashurbanipal, the Medes and Babylonians attacked Assyria from both the north and the south.

Assyria Falls
Assyria was like a wounded animal. Its massive structure was held together by sheer force. Enemies within and without circled the weakened giant hoping to bring it to its knees and destruction.

A relief from a palace at Nineveh shows King Ashurbanipal and his queen celebrating a victory over the king of Elam. The king's head hangs from a tree.

An Assyrian stele showing King Ashurbanipal carrying upon his head a basket filled with gifts.

A bloody and desperate battle was fought at Nineveh, after which the city finally fell in 612 B.C.E. and was completely destroyed by the victors.

The Battle of Megiddo / ca. 609 B.C.E.
In its final days, Assyria turned for help to Egypt, its old enemy and rival. Egypt's Pharaoh, Necho, prepared to take his army to Mesopotamia to aid the dying giant. He hoped that after he defeated Assyria's enemies he would be rewarded with a share of Assyria's territory. Confident that his armies would be able to pass freely through the lands which lay between him and the Assyrian forces, the ambitious Egyptian ruler began his march. But Josiah had no intention of allowing Egyptian soldiers to march unmolested through Judah, nor did he wish to see Assyria assisted.

Josiah summoned Judah's small army to halt the Egyptians. Although the Egyptian troops were superior both in numbers and arms, Josiah hoped that the high morale of his own soldiers would bring victory.

Josiah's army met the Egyptians at Megiddo, the gate to the plain of Jezreel and the site of many battles in the past. It was a bloody, desperate battle and Judah suffered a disastrous defeat. Josiah, the courageous king, perished at Megiddo with many of his brave men.

After Judah's defeat, Pharaoh Necho's army joined the Assyrian forces in Mesopotamia to fight for the city of Haran. But here the Medes and Babylonians were victorious, defeating Assyria and its Egyptian ally. Bitterly disappointed, the Pharaoh withdrew from Mesopotamia, and his army retreated through the lands which it had so recently conquered.

The Gladd Chronicle is a Babylonian clay tablet which recounts the battles of the Chaldean ruler Nabopolassar (625-605 B.C.E.) and his victories over Assyria.
The chronicle describes the capture of Nineveh by the Chaldeans and their allies the Medes, "They launched a powerful attack on the city and in the month of Abu the city was captured. They slaughtered the princes . . . They took much booty and turned the temple and the city into a ruin."

The Babylonian Empire

The Medes and the Babylonians divided the Assyrian Empire. The Medes took the territories in the north and the northeast; the Babylonians those in the south and southwest—the lands of the Fertile Crescent.

Judah the Vassal

In Judah, a sad time followed the death of King Josiah. After the defeat at Megiddo, Judah became a vassal of Egypt under Pharaoh Necho, a harsh master who forced it into utter submission. The reign of Josiah's son, Jehoahaz, lasted less than a year. He was taken captive to Egypt and died in exile. In 608 B.C.E., Necho appointed Jehoahaz's brother, Jehoiakim, as king of Judah. Jehoiakim was an obedient vassal. He installed Egyptian gods in Judah, followed Egypt's laws, and paid heavy tribute.

Belonging to Eliakim

Steward of Yaukin

The owner of this seal, Eliakim, was one of the officals of King Jehoiachin. "Yaukin" is one of the many variations of Jehoiakim's name.

Like a bone between two huge ferocious dogs, Judah found itself a small, weak nation with Egypt on one side and the advancing armies of Nebuchadnezzar of Babylon on the other. Fortunately for Judah, Nebuchadnezzar interrupted his victorious march when he received news of

A relief from Carchemish showing two heavily armed soldiers.

his aged father's death, returning to Babylon to receive homage as the new king. Thus little Judah was granted a brief time of peace.

Egypt now sought to undermine the power of Babylonia by encouraging its new vassals to revolt. King Jehoiakim of Judah, encouraged by Egyptian promises of assistance in case of a Babylonian attack, refused to pay tribute to Nebuchadnezzar. The Babylonian king promptly sent an army. but little Judah stood firm under Jehoiachin, who was only 18 years old when he succeeded his father, Jehoiakim.

Judah Invaded

Nebuchadnezzar himself finally took command of his troops, destroyed many cities of Judah, and marched up to the gates of Jerusalem. The promised Egyptian assistance never materialized, and in 597 B.C.E. Nebuchadnezzar took the city by storm, carrying young Jehoiachin and many important families into captivity.

One of a group of cuneiform texts listing the rations for captive kings and their retinues living in the vicinity of Babylon. Among the peoples listed are Philistines, Phoenicians, Judeans, Elamites, Medians, and Persians. These texts are basic for our knowledge of the treatment of captive foreigners by the Babylonians. This text is dated in the 13th year of Nebuchadnezzar II reign (592 B.C.E.). Jehoiachin and his sons are mentioned.

The First Exiles / ca. 597 B.C.E.

Judah's attempt to cast off the Babylonian yoke had only made matters worse. Jehoiachin was now exiled in Babylon along with many of his country's craftsmen, musicians, soldiers, and nobles.

Zedekiah, an uncle of Jehoiachin, another of Josiah's sons, ascended Judah's throne.

Zedekiah faced the same problem that had confronted his predecessors: should he rebel and shake off bondage, or should he allow Judah to remain a Babylonian vassal?

Most of the king's advisors favored rebellion, confident that Babylonia was not interested in further expansion. This confidence was strengthened by news reaching Judah that the captives in Babylon were being well treated. Unlike the Israelite captives in Assyria after the fall of Samaria, the exiles in Babylonia were not dispersed over various vassal lands, nor were they persecuted. Many of them had found useful employment and sent letters and messages home to their friends and relatives reporting how well they were faring. Encouraged by these stories, the members of Judah's war party urged Zedekiah to revolt.

An Assyrian relief showing Jewish prisoners of war playing lyres.

Jeremiah, Advocate of Peace

King Zedekiah / ca. 598–587 B.C.E.

Zedekiah had another advisor who urged him to cease all thought of revolt and devote himself solely to ensuring Judah's peace and welfare. This advisor was the aged prophet Jeremiah. Born in Anathoth, a small village near Jerusalem, Jeremiah was the son of a wealthy family of priests and had been given a good education. Before he received the call to prophecy he had lived a studious and quiet life. But the call to prophecy proved stronger than his misgivings, and Jeremiah, still a very young man, went forth to Jerusalem to declare the word of God.

Jeremiah had gone to the Temple of Jerusalem and prophesied that the House of God would be destroyed if the people did not willingly bear the Babylonian yoke. The people had been shocked by what seemed to them disloyalty, and Jeremiah became very unpopular. He was finally arrested and thrown into prison. After his release the prophet retired to his native town, Anathoth, with his loyal disciple Baruch.

Jeremiah in Disgrace

Baruch journeyed to Jerusalem to bring the words of the prophet to the king's attention. Jehoiakim refused to listen and scornfully burned the scrolls containing Jeremiah's message.

For ten years Judah had been wavering between revolt against Babylonia and peaceful acceptance of vassaldom. Zedekiah and his allies were about to decide in favor of revolt. Again the courageous Jeremiah raised his voice against this plan.

The people listened to the aged prophet when he appeared among them. He

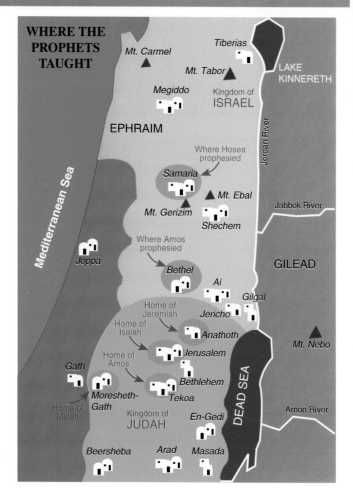

WHERE THE PROPHETS TAUGHT

warned that Judah was far too small and weak to challenge the mighty Babylonian empire. He begged them to preserve what freedom remained and comforted them by predicting that someday the captives would return from Babylon and Judah would be rebuilt.

Meanwhile, Egypt continued to support all efforts at revolt against Babylonia and sought allies for a last stand against the new empire.

When Judah's neighbors approached Zedekiah to form an alliance against Babylonia, he veered back to the side of the war party and began preparing his country for a long siege. Fortifications were strengthened, food and arms were stored, and all able-bodied men were trained for defense.

Jeremiah in Prison

In despair over these preparations for another war, the prophet Jeremiah renewed his warnings. He was denounced and again cast into prison.

An alliance was formed between Judah, Edom, Moab, Ammon, and the Phoenician cities of Tyre and Sidon. Pharaoh Apries of Egypt assured the allies of his support.

In the ninth year of his reign, after a long period of indecision, Zedekiah, the last king of Judah, revolted against Nebuchadnezzar of Babylon. The year was 586 B.C.E.

Judah Is Invaded Again

Nebuchadnezzar dealt swiftly with the rebellion. His army of charioteers, infantry, and cavalry far outnumbered the combined forces of the allies.

The Babylonian tidal wave rolled on to Jerusalem, the last fortified city of Judah. No help came from Judah's allies, for they were busy defending their own cities. The siege of Jerusalem began on the 10th day of Tevet in the year 586 B.C.E. It was briefly interrupted while Nebuchadnezzar marched off to do battle with the Egyptian army. When the Egyptians evaded him by retreating to their newly-won Phoenician ports, the Babylonians marched back to Judah and laid siege to Jerusalem once again.

Jerusalem Falls / ca. 586 B.C.E.

The people of Jerusalem valiantly defended their city against the battering rams, spears, and firebrands of the enemy. For 18 long months the walls around the city withstood the attack, but on the 10th day of Tammuz, the Babylonians managed to break through. After three more weeks of fighting, the Babylonians won a total victory. They destroyed the Temple and set fire to the rest of the city. The fateful day on which this tragic event occurred was the 9th of Av.

Zedekiah Captured / ca. 586 B.C.E.

On the 9th day of Av, Nebuchadnezzar entered Jerusalem in the morning, while his soldiers continued the destruction and plundering. Zedekiah was taken captive. He was forced to witness the death of his children. Then he was blinded and put in chains. Nearly all of the people of Judah were deported to Babylonia. By the end of the year the land of Judah was desolate. Its farms and vineyards lay barren. Its towns were in ruins.

With the fall of the kingdom of Judah, 400 years of rule by the House of David came to an end. Many more Judeans were deported to Babylonia in punishment of this violent act of rebellion.

Tisha Be-Av

The holiday of Tisha Be-Av is the saddest day of the Jewish year. On this day many Jewish tragedies took place. On the 9th of Av in 586 B.C.E., Solomon's Temple was destroyed; six centuries later in 70 C.E., on the same day, the Second Temple was destroyed; and in 1492 C.E., again on the same day, the Jews were driven out of Spain.

This miniature from a 14th century French Bible shows the blinded king Zedekiah being led into captivity. Zedekiah's desperate rebellion against Nebuchadnezzar led to the Babylonian invasion of Judah in 587 B.C.E.

Judah Falls / ca. 586 B.C.E.

Life In Babylonia

It is not difficult to imagine the homesickness and the bitter sorrow which must have filled the hearts of the exiles as they walked by the rivers of Babylon. The fame of Judah's musicians and singers had spread far and wide, and the Babylonians often asked the captives to sing them the songs of Zion. From the depths of their despair the exiles sang new songs, rising from glorious memories of desperate struggles of the past and the stark tragedy of the present:

If I forget thee, O Jerusalem,
Let my right hand forget her cunning
Let my tongue cleave to the roof of my
mouth
If I remember thee not: If I set not
Jerusalem
Above my chiefest joy. (Psalm 137)

Babylonia's most beautiful city was its capital, Babylon. Babylon was graced with paved streets, gardens, temples , and palaces. Even the city gates were adorned with multicolored, glazed bricks.This is a reconstruction of the Ishtar Gate in Babylon. The designs of lions, bulls, and dragons are made of baked bricks, covered with glazes of blue, gold, and white.

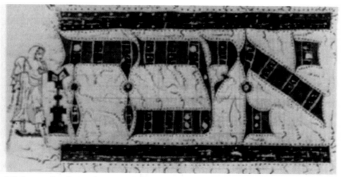

This painting from a German manuscript of 1344 decorates *Eycha*, the first Hebrew word in the Book of Lamentations. It shows a Jew, wearing a tallit, preparing to read the text.
The Book of Lamentations was written in response to the destruction of the First Temple. On Tisha Be-Av, it is read in the synagogue to a sad chant.

The exiles built a new life in Babylonia. Some continued to be farmers, others went to work on the irrigation and canal-digging projects which turned dry stretches of clay into fertile land. Most of the exiles, however, settled in the great cities of Babylonia, such as Babylon and Tel Abib.

From the many Babylonian records unearthed by archaeologists, we know that life in the Babylonian cities was on a high level of civilization. Among the records were found the books of a Jewish firm of merchants, Murashu and Sons, of the city of Nippur. These books were preserved in large clay jars much like those which held the Dead Sea Scrolls, written 600 years later. Judging from the records, Murashu and Sons was apparently known throughout Babylonia.

Jewish Observances in Babylonia

In the midst of Babylonia's strange and foreign ways, the Jewish exiles held fast to their own traditions. They kept to themselves in their own communities, observing the Sabbath, the holidays, and the religious laws. Each community conducted services in its own house of prayer. Precious Torah scrolls had been rescued from the destroyed cities of Judah, and from these the priests read portions from the ancient laws and history. Levites sang the old melodies, the psalms. Prophets spoke of God and gave renewed courage to the people. Thus did the exiles keep alive their faith and their traditions.

While the rulers and nobles of Babylon complacently admired their jewels and held feasts to honor their gods, the spirited young nation of Persia was on the march to the west, in the mountains of Iran. The Persians had been vassals of the Medes, but under the leadership of their young king, Cyrus, they gained their independence. Cyrus, the son of a Persian prince and a Median princess, was a brilliant and ambitious general.

The Handwriting on the Wall
As the rumble of Persian conquest grew louder, the rulers of the uneasy nations

The writing on a 5th century clay tablet from the city of Nippur. It is a rental agreement from the archives of the Jewish banking and commercial family Murashu. The language is primarily Babylonian with an Aramaic summary.

formed an alliance against Cyrus. He marched on to challenge the armies of Belshazzar, crown prince of Babylonia. The Bible records that during a feast, Belshazzar summoned Daniel, a Jewish seer, to interpret strange signs which had appeared on the wall of his palace. His most learned advisors had been unable to decipher this "handwriting on the wall," but Daniel explained that it foretold the conquest of Babylonia and the death of Belshazzar. And indeed, soon after Daniel's dire predictions, Belshazzar was murdered.

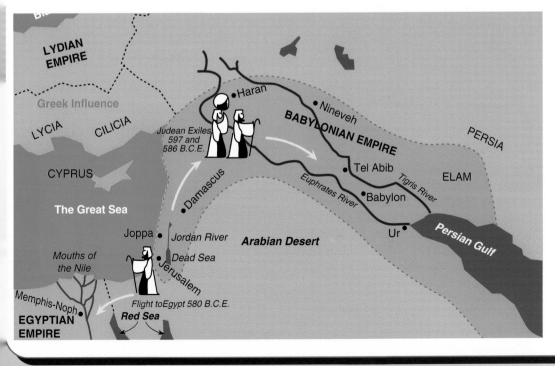

The route of the exiles to Babylon, following the destruction of the Temple in Jerusalem.

Cyrus, King of Persia

Cyrus the Conqueror / ca. 539 B.C.E.
Babylon's army was routed by the disciplined, well-organized Persian troops. The Babylonians fearfully awaited the plundering and devastation which they believed would inevitably follow. Cyrus, however, was unlike the conquerors of old. He entered the Babylonian capital with a minimum of harm to life and property. The entire ancient world marveled at the peaceful way in which this new lord took over the mighty Babylonian Empire.

Cyrus proved to be an efficient administrator and a monarch of great tolerance. He granted religious freedom to all, believing that a nation flourished best under such conditions. Many of the peoples of Babylonia regarded Cyrus as their liberator. Under his rule, Persia became a great nation.

The armies of Babylon were defeated by the Persians. The Persians were good to the Jews. They allowed Ezra and many Jews to return to Judea. Persian soldiers escorted the Jews. These are Persian soldiers. They are armed with spears and bows.

The Persian conquest of Babylonia in 539 B.C.E. was a great boon for the Jewish exiles. Cyrus was sympathetic to them and soon issued a decree permitting them to return to Jerusalem and restore their Temple. Great was the rejoicing in the Jewish communities. Scores of exiles prepared to make the long-dreamed-of journey back to their homeland.

From the biblical Book of Ezra we learn that about 42,000 Jews from all over Babylonia joined in the exodus to Judah. Their long, difficult journey took them through the lands of the Fertile Crescent, retracing Abraham's trek of ancient days.

Inscribed cylinder recording the capture of Babylon by Cyrus. It tells how "without battle and without fighting Marduk (the god of Babylon) made him (Cyrus) enter into his city of Babylon; he spared Babylon tribulation, and Nabonidus the (Chaldean) king, who feared him not, he delivered into his hand." Nabonidus, the Chaldean king of Babylon, was not in favor with the priests, and they assisted in delivering the city to Cyrus.

The Exiles

The Second Commonwealth / ca. 520 B.C.E.

The land of Judah lay barren. Fields and vineyards were deserted; villages and towns were in ruins. Jerusalem was a city of desolation. The magnificent Temple of Solomon had been destroyed, and grass was growing on its site.

The pioneers from Babylonia wasted no time lamenting the past. All their energy was needed now for rebuilding. Amid the ruins of the Temple they erected an altar for the worship of God. They plowed the barren fields and tended the cattle they had brought with them. They were joyfully assisted in their labors by the few Jews who had escaped deportation and had remained in Judah, living in great poverty in the hills, where they had fled for safety.

The head of the community was Zerubbabel, a prince of the House of David. Zerubbabel had led the returning pioneers back to their land and was appointed governor by Cyrus. The priest Joshua, son of an ancient priestly family, assisted Zerubbabel. The Second Commonwealth, founded by the returning Babylonian exiles, was called Judea.

When Assyria conquered the northern kingdom of Israel and deported most of its people, a small number of Jews had managed to remain there. They had intermarried with the non-Jewish newcomers whom the Assyrians had settled in the territory around Samaria. Their descendants were called Samaritans. The Samaritans considered themselves Israelites, but followed some of the customs of their non-Jewish ancestors. When they learned of the exiles' return, they wanted to be part of the new commonwealth and offered to help rebuild the Temple.

The tomb of Cyrus, who allowed the Jews to return to Jerusalem.

The newly returned pioneers feared that the Samaritans might introduce idolatrous ways and even bring idols into the new Temple.

THE RESTORATION

Cyrus was a liberal ruler and allowed the worship of the God of Israel in Jerusalem.

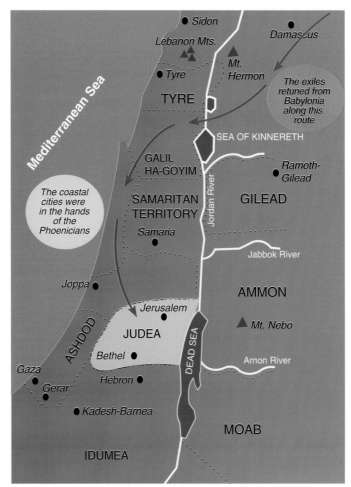

The Samaritans

The Samaritans Accuse the Jews

The Samaritans were bitterly offended by the Jews' refusal of their assistance. They subsequently built a temple of their own on Mount Gerizim and worshipped in their own territory. Thenceforth the two peoples were enemies.

The Samaritans sought to hinder the Jews from rebuilding the Temple in Jerusalem. They wrote to the government in Persia, false claiming that the Jews were planning to revolt and persuading King Cambyses II, the son of Cyrus, to put a stop to the reconstruction.

In their despair the Judeans turned to their prophets. The prophets bade them be of good faith, foretelling that the building of the Temple would be resumed soon—even in their own day. For several years no further work was done on the Temple, for the Jews dared not defy the order of the Persian king. During these years the prophets Haggai and Zechariah

were a source of great help and strength to the community.

Darius Encourages the Jews

When Darius (522–486 B.C.E.) succeeded to the throne, the Jews sent letters of petition

Mosaic in an ancient Samaritan synagogue, showing the Greek influence.

to the new king. Darius considered their case. Upon reading the original decree issued by Cyrus, he declared the Jews innocent of the charge brought against them and sent messengers to encourage the building of the Temple.

Unfortunately, the Samaritans were not the only enemies of the Jews. Edomites,

The Torah of the Samaritans is housed in the synagogue in Nablus. It is written in ancient Hebrew and is extremely old.

Page from Samaritan Bible. Damascus, 1485.

King Darius of Persia (521–486 B.C.E.), seated on the throne; his son Xerxes stands behind in attendance.

Moabites, and Ammonites attacked the poorly-armed settlers. Raiding parties seized their meager harvests and attacked their homes.

Despite these harassments the Jews toiled on. They worked night and day, living in poor huts and sparing time from the building only to provide the barest necessities of food and clothing for themselves.

In comparison to the magnificent Temple of Solomon, the new Temple was unimposing indeed. However, the Levites sang the same sacred old melodies and the priests offered the same prayers and sacrifices as they had in the First Temple. Again, the people came and assembled in the courts to worship.

The task of reconstructing the Temple completed, the people could now turn to the rebuilding of the land.

Cylinder seal with the name of Darius in three languages, Persian, Assyrian, and Scythian.

A gold coin (daric) named after Darius I. Darics continued to be minted under Alexander and his successors. This coin is dated to the 4th century B.C.E.

Rebuilding the Temple / *ca. 458–445 B.C.E.*

Ezra the Scribe

Among the Jews in Babylonia who were distressed by the news of Judea's troubled state was Ezra, a learned Jew of priestly descent. Ezra was a dedicated teacher and had many disciples whom he instructed in the Torah. Because he was highly skilled in the art of writing Torah scrolls, he is often referred to as Ezra the Scribe (Ezra Hasofer).

When Ezra applied to King Artaxerxes I for permission to go to Jerusalem with his disciples, his request was granted. The king and the Jewish community of Babylonia generously gave Ezra many gifts for the Temple and also the supplies he needed for the long journey.

Approximately 1,500 Jews, eager to return to their homeland, accompanied Ezra to Judea. They arrived in Jerusalem in the summer of 458 B.C.E. and were warmly welcomed by the people of Judea, who

Hebrew coin dating back to the 4th century B.C.E, the period of Ezra the Scribe. The coin is inscribed *YHD* (in ancient Hebrew script), which stands for Yehud, the Persian name of Judea.

had gone forth to meet the new group of pioneers.

Ezra began his task without delay. He traveled through the land visiting and teaching, but was saddened and disturbed to find among most of the people a lack of knowledge of the Torah.

Patiently, he reasoned with them, reminding them of their great struggle to regain their homeland and their high purpose in doing so. A great many were deeply impressed by Ezra's words and promised to give up the heathen ways which were undermining their character.

Nehemiah, Governor of Judea / ca. 445 B.C.E.

The next major task was to fortify Jerusalem against the hostile bands of raiders by rebuilding the city's walls. Building fortifications, however, would make the Persians suspicious and open the Judeans to the charge of planning a revolt.

In this relief from a palace in Persepolis Phoenicians are presenting tribute to a Persian king.

Help came in 445 B.C.E. when Nehemiah, a Babylonian Jew, was appointed governor of Judea. Nehemiah had been the trusted cupbearer of King Artaxerxes I in Shushan (Susa), the Persian capital.

The two great leaders, Ezra and Nehemiah, combined their efforts to restore the commonwealth of Judea. Ezra was Judea's spiritual guide; Nehemiah, the governor, was its political leader. Inspired by Nehemiah, the people set about rebuilding the walls of Jerusalem with great enthusiasm.

"Come," they said, "let us go and rebuild the walls of Jerusalem. Let us end our shame. We shall work in the daytime and stand watch during the night."

The walls and fortifications were completed in just 52 days. The men of Judea defended the walls fiercely, and the raiders soon began to think twice before they attacked.

The tomb of Darius I at Naqsh-i-Roustem, Persia.

The Commonwealth of Judea

Nehemiah was well versed in Jewish law, and with the help of Ezra he laid the foundations of the new Jewish commonwealth. The Torah was its constitution, the fundamental law of Judea. Ezra and his disciples, traveling among the people, instructed them in Torah and saw to it that they lived by their own laws and not by those of their heathen neighbors or of Persia.

The new commonwealth of Judea began to thrive. Farmers and shepherds harvested in peace and took their oil and wool, their fruits and grain to the market in Jerusalem. Traders came again from the neighboring countries to sell their wares in the city.

The Festival of Sukkot

Ezra and Nehemiah together brought about the political reconstruction and spiritual rejuvenation of Judea. On the day before the festival of Sukkot in the year 445 B.C.E., numerous Judeans made their way to Jerusalem. They assembled in the ancient City of David and built their tabernacles. The people gathered to hear the proclamations of their two great leaders. Nehemiah and the priests and Levites of the Temple stood before the assembled Judeans while Ezra read to them from the Torah.

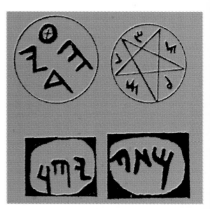

Official seals of the province of Judah during the 5th-4th centuries B.C.E.

The Spiritual Revival

Ezra and his disciples continued their travels through the land. They carried Torah scrolls with them and taught not only the judges in the courts but everyone who wanted to learn. During this time a new way of writing Hebrew was adopted. The ancient Hebrew script was replaced by one very much like the Hebrew script we use today.

Ever since the time of Moses and Joshua, a body of unwritten interpretations of the Torah, known as the Oral Tradition, had been handed down by the elders, prophets, and scribes. The Oral Tradition was revived by Ezra and his disciples. After the time of Ezra, it continued to be passed down from generation to generation by word of mouth. Over the years, many new interpretations were added, since each generation applied the Torah to its own times and its own problems. This process culminated many centuries later when the Oral Tradition was put into writing in the Mishnah, Talmud, and Midrash.

The Synagogue

The work of Ezra and Nehemiah was followed by an era of peace for Judea. Towns and villages were rebuilt; land was tilled and cultivated. Many towns built their own small marketplaces and houses of prayer. The latter, which grew into the institution that we now refer to as the synagogue, were the centers of communal life. In them the priests and scribes taught the Torah and led the people in observing the festivals. Here the people met to celebrate Sabbaths and holidays, to conduct meetings and discuss community problems. Here judges held court and marriages were celebrated.

In the course of centuries, especially after the destruction of the Second Temple, the synagogue became the heart of every Jewish community. It was a place where strangers could seek shelter, where the poor received alms, and where those with problems or disputes could come for counsel.

Modern Hebrew	Old Hebrew	Phoenician	Early Greek	Later Greek	Latin	English
א	—	—	A	A	A	A
ב	—	—	—	B	B	B
ג	—	—	—	—	C G	C G
ד	—	—	—	—	D	D
ה	—	—	—	—	E	E
ו	—	—	—	—	F V	F V U
ז	—	—	—	—	—	Z
ח	—	—	—	—	H	E H
ט	—	—	—	—	—	TH PH
י	—	—	—	—	I	I
כ	—	—	—	—	—	K KH
ל	—	—	—	—	L	L
מ	—	—	—	—	M	M
נ	—	—	—	—	N	N
ס	—	—	—	—	X	X
ע	—	—	—	—	O	O
פ	—	—	—	—	P	P
צ	—	—	—	—	—	S
ק	—	—	—	—	Q	Q
ר	—	—	—	—	R	R
ש	—	—	—	—	S	S
ת	—	—	—	—	T	T

Table showing how the Hebrew and Phoenician letters passed through Greek and Latin forms to their present English forms.

The Targum

Throughout the Near East, and especially in Babylonia and Syria, Aramaic was the dominant language. After the return from the Babylonian exile, it also became the everyday spoken language of Judea. Since the Torah was written in Hebrew, it was necessary to provide a translation for the many people who were no longer able to understand it.

Ezra solved the problem by providing a translator who stood right next to the Torah reader during services and translated the Hebrew into Aramaic for the congregants. Eventually the oral translations provided in this manner were set down in writing. The Aramaic translation of the Torah is called the Targum. Note the close similarly between the name Targum and the word *meturgeman* (translator).

The Talmud mentions that in some synagogues the Torah was read twice, once in Hebrew and once in Aramaic.

There are three major Aramaic translations of the Torah: Targum Onkelos, Targum Jonathan, and the Palestinian Targum (Targum Yerushalmi).

Page from a Hebrew Bible with commentaries. The narrow column at the upper left is the Aramaic translation by Onkelos, the most widely-used Targum. It is still printed side by side with the original Hebrew text in modern editions of the Torah. Some Jews recite it with the regular weekly portion. Onkelos was a convert to Judaism.

A page from the Palestinian Targum of the Torah. This translation may have originated in the Second Temple period. It was lost, until a copy was discovered in the Vatican Library. This page contains Genesis 4:14-5:1.

The Story of Purim / *ca. 486–465 B.C.E.*

Persia was a generous ruler. Although Judea was a province of the Persian Empire, it was allowed to govern itself. During this period, the Jews of Babylonia also fared well under Persian control.

A dramatic glimpse of Jewish life under Persian rule is provided by the biblical story of Esther, which took place in Shushan (Susa), the capital of Persia, in 486–485 B.C.E. The king in the story is named Ahasuerus, probably a form of Xerxes. According to the Bible, his kingdom extended from Ethiopia to India and he ruled over 127 provinces.

Mordecai Defies Haman

Ahasuerus asked his wife, Vashti, to dance for the drunken guests at a palace party. When she refused, he decided to punish her disobedience by finding a new queen. A beauty contest was held to choose a successor; the winner was a Jewish girl named Esther. Her uncle Mordecai was an employee of the king.

The names Mordecai and Esther are similar to the Persian names Marduk and Ishtar. The fact that the Jews of Persia had Persian names, just as Jews in America today have English names, shows that they

This gold cup with a lion base is from the 5th and 6th century. Such cups were in use during the reign of Xerxes.

A fresco found at the 3rd century Dura Europos synagogue shows Ahasuerus and Esther. The king is being given a letter by one of his attendants. Esther, the queen, is seated on the throne to the king's left. Esther's head is covered with a tall crown

The palaces of the Persian kings were very large and ornate. Archaeologists at Persepolis have uncovered several stone palaces dating from the time of Darius and Xerxes. This is the Hall of Pillars with its 72 giant pillars. It is calculated that it was large enough to accommodate 10,000 celebrants.

were fully assimilated into the nonreligious aspects of the dominant culture.

Sometime after this, Mordecai refused to bow down to Haman, the king's grand vizier. Haman was very angry; he went to Ahasuerus and accused the Jews of plotting against the government.

He said, "Their laws are different, and they do not obey the king's rulings. If it pleases the king, let them be destroyed." Just as the Nazis tried to destroy all the Jews in Europe, Haman wanted to wipe out all the Jews in the Persian Empire. Ahasuerus agreed to his proposal.

Esther Saves the Jews

When Mordecai found out about the impending pogrom against the Jews of Persia, he urged Esther to save her people. Bravely violating a law that prohibited anyone from approaching the king without an invitation, Esther went to Ahasuerus. She revealed that she was Jewish and that Haman's bloodthirsty plot would destroy her people. The king ordered Haman hanged on the very gallows he had built for Mordecai. He appointed Mordecai one of his advisors and as a token of trust gave him Haman's signet ring. The Jews of Persia were given permission to defend themselves against their enemies. The holiday of Purim was instituted to commemorate this series of events.

The Holiday of Purim

Jews all over the world celebrate Purim by reading the story of brave Queen Esther in the Megillah. They exchange *shalah manot* gifts and sing and dance and conduct masquerades.

The name Purim comes from the Hebrew word *pur,* meaning "lot." Haman set the day for the pogrom against the Jews by casting lots (*purim*). Purim, the Feast of Lots, is celebrated on the 14th day of the Hebrew month of Adar.

Persia Falls

Far to the west of Shushan, a great civilization, with its center in Athens, was growing up in Greece. Perhaps inevitably, the Greeks and the Persians came into conflict. In the 5th century B.C.E. Persia invaded Greece.

Although the Persians were defeated at Marathon and Salamis, their resources were so huge that they continued the struggle even after their armies withdrew, using their vast wealth to bribe Greek traitors and finance wars among the Greek city-states.

An 18th century, artistically illustrated Scroll of Esther (Megillah) from Alsace, France.

Timeline—The Age of the Tanak

JEWISH HIGHLIGHTS

Patriarchs and Matriarchs
2000–1700 B.C.E.

Israelites in Egypt
1720–1280 B.C.E.

Exodus from Egypt
1280 B.C.E.

The Desert
1280–1240 B.C.E.

Promised Land
1240–1080 B.C.E.

King Saul
1020–1004 B.C.E.

King David
1004–965 B.C.E.

JEWISH • EVENTS PERSONALITIES • LITERATURE • HOLIDAYS

Patriarchs and Matriarchs	Israelites in Egypt	Exodus from Egypt	The Desert	Promised Land	King Saul	King David
One God	Joseph	Moses / Aaron / Miriam	Shavuot / Sukkot / Ark of the Covenant / Tabernacle	Joshua / Judges / Twelve tribes	Samuel the Priest	Jerusalem capital
Ivrim–Hebrews	Moses	Sea of Reeds	Ten Commandments	Deborah	Saul unites tribes	Ark to Jerusalem
Promised Land Canaan	Children of Israel	Passover	Torah	Gideon	Jonathan	Psalms of David
			Mount Sinai	Samson	David	Bathsheba
				Samuel		

WORLD HISTORY

Patriarchs and Matriarchs	Israelites in Egypt	Exodus from Egypt	The Desert	Promised Land	King Saul	King David
Hittites	Hyksos	Merneptah	Babylon	Canaanites	Aram	Philistines
Hammurabi	Rameses II			Medianites	Damascus	
Babylon	Assyria			Philistines		

*All dates are approximate

Timeline—The Age of the Tanak

JEWISH HIGHLIGHTS

King Solomon
965–926 B.C.E.

Division of Israel and Judah
928 B.C.E.

House of Omri
871–845 B.C.E.

Fall of Israel
721 B.C.E.

Fall of Judea
586 B.C.E.

Ezra and Nehemiah
460–515 B.C.E.

Queen Esther
486–465 B.C.E.

JEWISH EVENTS • PERSONALITIES • LITERATURE • HOLIDAYS

King Solomon	Division of Israel and Judah	House of Omri	Fall of Israel	Fall of Judea	Ezra and Nehemiah	Queen Esther
SOLOMON builds First Temple	Rehoboam Jeroboam	Ahab	Hosea	ISAIAH	Temple rebuilt	Purim
Queen of Sheba	Egypt attacks Israel	Jezebel	Amos	Micah	Hebrew language	Mordecai
		Athaliah	Ten lost tribes	Jeremiah	Jewish Commonwealth	Haman
		Elijah		King Zedekiah	First synagogues	Ahasuerus
		Elisha		Tisha Be-Av	Bible completed	
					Samaritans	

WORLD HISTORY

Hiram of Tyre	Assyria	Assyria	Assyria	Egypt	Cyrus	Persia
	Egypt	Aram	Sargon	Medes	Artaxerxes	Xerxes
	Shishak	Phoenicia	Tiglath Pileser III	Assyria	Samaritans	Darius
			Shalmaneser V	Babylon	Persia	
				Esarhaddon		
				Nebuchadnezzar		
				Sennacherib		

Alexander the Great / ca. 336–323 BCE

The Macedonians

A new threat loomed in Macedonia, the rugged country to the north of Greece. Under King Philip, the Macedonians conquered Greece. Philip's son, known to history as Alexander the Great (356–323 B.C.E.), set out to conquer the sprawling and unbelievably wealthy Persian Empire.

A mosaic showing a likeness of Alexander the Great.

Alexander was a brilliant general. In the next few years he conquered all the Persian lands---a vast territory that included the modern countries of Turkey, Syria, Israel, Egypt, Iraq, and Iran---and pushed on into Arabia, Afghanistan, and Pakistan. When his troops marched into Judea in 332 B.C.E., Alexander was kind to its people, for he knew that the Jews had a remarkable civilization of their own, and he loved and respected culture and scholarship.

Alexander founded many cities in the territories he conquered. The most famous of these was Alexandria in Egypt. Built on the Nile delta, Alexandria became a great trading port and center of Greek culture. People from Judea were invited to settle there, and from then on Jews always constituted a substantial part of its population.

The Empire Is Divided

Alexander's huge empire was destined to be short-lived, for the young ruler died of a fever in 323 B.C.E., when he was only 33 years old. His three most powerful generals conspired against his heirs and brutally murdered them. One of the generals, Antigonus, took over Macedonia and Greece. Another, Seleucus, took Babylon, Persia, Syria, and the adjoining territories. The third, Ptolemy, ruled over Egypt.

The Jews of Alexandria

Judea was part of Ptolemy's kingdom and remained under Egyptian rule for a century. A flourishing Jewish community developed in Alexandria, the most important city of the Ptolemaic kingdom. Jewish settlers had helped to build the city, and Alexander had granted them the same rights and privileges as its Greek citizens. Jews flocked to Alexandria from other parts of Egypt and from the rugged Judean hills. In this city on the Mediterranean coast, they found not only new opportunities but a new way of life.

Alexander the Great being greeted by the high priest Jaddua. From a 14th century French picture.

Under the rule of the Ptolemies, Alexandria became one of the most important cities of the ancient world. Although the Jews of Alexandria practiced their own religion and conducted their own communal life in their synagogues, they were attracted to the ways of the Greeks. They adopted the Greek language, and many took part in Greek sports and debates. For centuries the Jews of Alexandria had to wrestle with one of the gravest problems facing Jews of their era: Greek civilization versus the Jewish way of life.

The Ptolemies were kind to the Jews, and for more than 100 years Judea was at peace under the protection of Egypt. The Ptolemies did not demand unreasonable taxes and seldom interfered with the Judean government.

A reconstruction of the famous lighthouse in the harbor of Alexandria.

Mosaic found at Pompei records the battle of Issus between the Macedonians and the Persians. Alexander the Great, bareheaded (at left), charges the bodyguard surrounding the Persian king, Darius III.

The Septuagint / *ca. 285–246 B.C.E.*

The Bible in Greek / ca. 285–246 B.C.E.

Under Ptolemy II Philadelphus, the Bible was translated into Greek. This came about, we are told, because the library at Alexandria had a copy of every book in the world except the Bible. Wanting its collection to be complete, Ptolemy sent to Jerusalem for a Bible and asked the high priest for permission to have it translated. He invited 72 Jewish sages to Alexandria and set each of them to work by himself. The 72 sages had no contact with one another, but when they finished, all 72 translations were identical. We do not know whether this story is fact or legend, but whatever may be the case, the first Greek translation of the Bible came to be known as the Septuagint, meaning the translation "by the seventy."

The Septuagint created a great stir. By that time Greek had become the most widely used language in the ancient world.

A page from the Septuagint, Exodus 19.

The Septuagint translation also enabled non-Jews to read the Bible. Before long the entire ancient world became acquainted with the history and ideas of the people of the little land of Judea. Many non-Jews, known as "God-fearers," began attending synagogues or adopting Jewish customs.

Bust of Ptolemy IV (285–246 B.C.E.)

Many Jews in Egypt and other countries no longer knew Hebrew. Their knowledge of Judaism had suffered as a result, but now they were able to read the Holy Scriptures and study the laws of the Torah.

Oval containing the name "Ptolemy" in hieroglyphics.

Torah Prophetic History—Tanak

In Judea itself, the people continued to live peacefully, abiding by the laws of the Torah as explained by the high priest and by the members of the Great Assembly. The Torah was not a secret book to be read only by scholars. It was the law and the way of life for the entire nation. Almost all Jews could read and write, and beginning in the time of Ezra, the Torah was studied in depth by people of every background—farmers and shepherds, merchants and artisans. The scribes, teachers, and scholars who made up the Great Assembly were not a tiny elite, but represented the entire populace.

When necessary, the Great Assembly interpreted the laws of the Torah to fit new conditions and situations. This body, known also as the Great Synagogue and as the Sanhedrin, was at one and the same time a legislature, a court, and a national council. In addition, it served as a training ground for the leaders who went out to teach in the synagogues of Judea's towns and villages.

The Bible Is Compiled / ca. 200 B.C.E.

The scribes collected and carefully examined all the holy writings. These were put together in the great collection of sacred literature that eventually came to be known as the Hebrew Bible. Among the writings they included were the Five Books of Moses, or Torah; the books of the prophets; historical works like the books of Samuel, Kings, Chronicles, Ezra, Nehemiah, Esther, and Ruth; and philosophical and poetic works like Psalms, Lamentations, Ecclesiastes, Job, and Proverbs.

The Bible was the repository of the Jewish historical and religious experience, the highpoint of ancient Hebrew literary achievement, and the foundation of Judaism. In addition to the writings gathered in the Bible, many other books were written in Hebrew throughout this period. Some of them were lost with the passage of time. Others were preserved in later collections such as the Apocrypha.

GENESIS
EXODUS
LEVITICUS
NUMBERS
DEUTERONOMY

Note: except for TORAH books with the same color are counted as one unit.

PROPHETS

JOSHUA
JUDGES
1 SAMUEL
2 SAMUEL
1 KINGS
2 KINGS
ISAIAH
JEREMIAH
EZEKIEL
HOSEA
JOEL
AMOS
OBADIAH
JONAH
MICAH
NAHUM
HABAKKUK
ZEPHANIAH
HAGGAI
ZECHARIAH
MALACHI

12 minor prophets

WRITINGS

PSALMS
PROVERBS
JOB
SONG OF SOLOMON
RUTH
LAMENTATIONS
ECCLESIASTES
ESTHER
DANIEL
EZRA
NEHEMIAH
1 CHRONICLES
2 CHRONICLES

THE TANAK (BIBLE)

The complete Hebrew Bible is called TaNaK. It is divided into three divisions; Torah (Five Books of Moses), Neviim (Prophets), and Ketuvim (Writings).

The name Tanak comes from the first letters of each of the three divisions. *T* is for Torah, *N* is for Neviim and *K* is for Ketuvim.

There are a total of 24 separate books in the Tanak. The Torah consists of 5 books, the Prophets 8 books, and the Writings 11 books.

The chapter divisions and the numbering of the verses were introduced into the Tanak to make quoting from it much easier.

The language of the Tanak is Hebrew except for portions of the books of Daniel and Ezra, which are in Aramaic.

The Seleucids Rule Israel / ca. 198 B.C.E.

The Seleucid kings of Syria sought to win Palestine from the Ptolemies of Egypt. After many battles the Syrian king Antiochus III defeated Ptolemy V of Egypt in 198 B.C.E. Antiochus III reduced taxes and guaranteed that Jewish religious law would be respected. When his son, Antiochus IV, ascended the throne in 175 B.C.E., conditions worsened, for he doubled the tax burden on Judea and abused the Jewish religion.

A bust of Antiochus III (223–187 B.C.E.)

A Greek inscription from a Jerusalem synagogue, in the time of Herod. The inscription reads: "Theodotus, priest and leader of the synagogue, built it to recite the Torah and study the commandments . . . and the water system for the comfort (of strangers)."

Hellenism and Judaism

Gradually, the people of Judea divided into two factions. Those who adopted the Greek way of life and Greek religious practices were called Hellenists. The majority who continued to adhere to the laws of the Torah were called Hasidim ("pious ones"). Whereas the Hellenists were willing to abandon Judaism in order to be accepted by their pagan rulers, the Hasidim adhered to the traditional Jewish ideal of living as servants of the one invisible God—acting justly, showing mercy, and obeying the commandments of the Torah.

The Seleucid kings were Greeks, and like the Ptolemies of Egypt, they promoted and spread Greek culture. Antiochus took steps to induce the Jews to adopt Greek customs. All the important government posts went to those who complied. Before long, Greek ideas and the Greek way of life had become very fashionable among many of Judea's wealthy nobles and merchants.

Bronze bust of Seleucus I which was found near Pompeii, Italy.

Judaism Threatened

The Greek way of life opened the doors to a new world for the affluent pleasure-seekers who adopted it. Many Judeans were willing to cast aside their ancient traditions and lose themselves in the new life. The conflict between the Hellenists, who advocated assimilation to Greek paganism, and the Hasidim, who upheld the ways of Judaism, was a bitter one.

Judaism was threatened abroad as well as at home. Because Judea was a small country that could not support a large population, many of its people had left their homeland and settled in other countries. Known collectively as the Jews of the Diaspora (Dispersion), they were exposed to strong Greek cultural influences in the cities where they lived. In Alexandria and other places, many of them adopted Greek as their primary language. Knowledge of Hebrew began to die out. Although the majority remained committed to Judaism, they were unable to study the Torah, a serious problem that was finally solved by the Septuagint translation of the Bible.

The Hasidim

The Hasidim believed that Greek paganism and social practices would lead to immorality. Greek idol worship, love of conflict, and tolerance of drunkenness would weaken the Jewish way of life. At times there were violent confrontations between Hasidim and Hellenists.

The most extreme Hellenists urged their fellow Jews to use the Greek language and worship Greek gods.

A Greek relief of naked wrestlers at a gymnasium. The gymnasiun was a sport stadium where games and concerts were held. Before an exhibition there was a special opening ceremony in which the athletes paraded naked and then offered sacrifices to the pagan gods.
To the Greeks, it was a way of life. To the Jews, it was a road to idol worship and assimilation.

The Reign of Antiochus IV / ca. 175–163 B.C.E.

The situation came to a head during the reign of Antiochus IV. He hoped to build his kingdom into a great power, but his dreams were threatened by a new empire rising in the west.

The Romans had conquered Greece and Macedonia and marched on to Asia Minor. The Seleucid army was unable to stop them, and as a result Antiochus lost some of his western territories to Rome.

In order to raise funds to defend his kingdom against the growing Roman threat, Antiochus imposed high taxes on Judea to help defray the expense of hiring mercenary soldiers, equipping his vast army, and maintaining his splendid court at Antioch, the Syrian capital.

In addition, Antiochus humiliated the Jews by placing a statue of himself in the Temple.

Antiochus and the Jewish Religion / ca. 168 B.C.E.

Eventually, Antiochus outlawed Judaism altogether. It became a serious offense to observe Jewish laws. The Torah was a forbidden book; the Sabbath, festivals, and holy days could no longer be celebrated in public.

Antiochus added the Greek word Epiphanes ("God made manifest") to his name. Many Judeans, however, referred to him as Antiochus Epimanes—"Antiochus the Madman." Although Antiochus had proclaimed himself a god and decreed that those who opposed him would die, many brave men and women in Judea refused to pay homage at the Greek shrines.

The Maccabees

The first stirrings of revolt came in the village of Modin, near Jerusalem. Syrian officials and soldiers had come to Modin to collect taxes and force the people to worship the Greek gods. There was an old priest in the village, a man called Mattathias, of the Hasmonean family. Mattathias, surrounded by his five sons, walked up to the heathen altar. A Jew who collaborated with the Syrians had just bowed to the idols. Mattathias raised his sword high and his voice came out loud and clear:

"He who is with God, let him come to me!" he cried, and slew the traitorous idol worshipper.

The old priest's bold act inspired his sons and followers. They fell upon the Syrian soldiers and officials and killed them. Only a few escaped.

The Revolt Begins

The long-awaited revolt had begun! News of the incident at Modin spread like wildfire until all Judea was inflamed. Mattathias, his sons, and their followers fled to the mountains and joined forces with the Hasidim.

Marble bust of Antiochus IV (175–163 B.C.E.)

Statue of Zeus (Jupiter) found at Caesarea. Throughout Judea, Syrian overlords forced the Jews to worship before such idols at public altars.

A Greek soldier under attack. He wears a metal helmet and breastplate. This painting was found on an ancient stone coffin.

Mattathias died soon after the beginning of the revolt, but his five sons—Judah, Yohanan, Simon, Eliezer, and Jonathan—took over. The commander was Judah, who was called HaMakkabi, "the Hammerer." The letters of his name are said to have stood for the rebels' password and battle-cry: *Mi kamokah ba'elim, Adonai!* ("Who is like you among the gods, O Lord!").

The people of Judea rallied to the cause of the sons of Mattathias, now known as the Maccabees. In 1995 a road-building crew near Modin uncovered several tombs. Israeli archaeologists are excavating and cataloguing the objects in the tombs.

These newly discovered tombs were discovered while expanding a highway in the vicinity of Modin, ancestral home of the Maccabees. The Hebrew sign indicates that this dig is sponsored by the Israel Department of Antiquities.

The Battle for Freedom / ca. 168–165 B.C.E.

Although the revolutionary movement in Judea was growing day by day, Antiochus refused to take it seriously. He felt sure that his highly trained, well-equipped army could handle any threat.

An enameled picture of Judah Maccabee. It was painted in the 15th century by a French artist.

Judah Maccabee, an able general and a fine strategist, avoided an open battle with the main Syrian forces. Biding his time, he conducted a classic guerilla campaign, striking here and there, attacking whenever feasible. He defeated a Syrian unit based in Samaria and later ambushed a sizable Syrian column passing through the narrow pass of Beth-Horon. The Syrians, taken by surprise, were routed. They fled in wild disorder, leaving their weapons and equipment behind.

Judah Maccabee's Army

Judah Maccabee's army consisted of 6,000 untrained men armed only with equipment taken from the enemy and a few weapons made in Judea's crude forges. But the rebels had two advantages over the Syrians. First, they knew the terrain, since it was their homeland. Second,

they were fighting for a prize of untold value—their religion. They were determined to make a firm stand against the enemy no matter what the cost.

Still avoiding open battle, Judah and 3,000 men made a surprise attack at night on the Syrian encampment at Emmaus. Unable to rally in time, the Syrians again took flight. Their losses were heavy and their camp went up in flames. The Jews had won another great victory against overwhelming odds.

The Temple Is Restored

Now the triumphant Jews marched on Jerusalem. A dismaying sight greeted them, for the Temple was defiled by dirt and refuse and desecrated by idolatrous images.

Together, the victorious Jews set about cleaning their house of worship. Judah Maccabee and his men were assisted in this task by the priests and by the people of Jerusalem.

A Syrian war elephant. These huge beasts with sharp-shooting bowmen were the armored tanks of the ancient world.

Joyfully the army of cleaners and polishers worked, erecting a new altar to the one God in order to rededicate themselves to their faith.

The Miracle of Hanukkah / 165 B.C.E.

On the 25th day of Kislev, 165 B.C.E., three years after its desecration, the Temple was rededicated. The golden Menorah was lit once more. The Temple Menorah had only seven branches. It may still be seen today, in a relief on the Arch of Titus in Rome and on the official emblem of the State of Israel.

Tradition tells us that the victors found only enough oil in the Temple to keep the Eternal Light burning for one day. Yet miraculously the golden Menorah burned for eight full days. The eight-branched menorah of today and the annual eight-day celebration of Hanukkah, the Festival of Lights, commemorate the victory won for freedom by Judah Maccabee and his courageous followers.

Aware that the Seleucid state was still strong enough to threaten Judea, Judah Maccabee shrewdly decided to make a pact with Rome. For a time, this kept the Syrians at bay, for they were afraid to attack an ally of a power as mighty as Rome. Gradually, however, this fear lessened and Syria again invaded Judea, regaining some of its old strongholds.

Death of Judah Maccabee

The Syrians did not win all the battles, however, for Judah Maccabee defeated the Seleucid elephant corps near Beth-Horon. A month later, however, the Syrians returned with a fresh army of 22,000 men. Against this overwhelming force Judah Maccabee pitted an army of 800. Sheer bravery was not enough and the Judeans suffered a grave defeat.

Judea suffered a terrible loss; Judah Maccabee fell in battle. The beloved leader was carried home to Modin by his retreating soldiers and laid to rest beside his father.

Despite the loss of their great warrior leader, the Judeans stubbornly refused to submit to Syrian rule. Death had now taken all but two of the five brave brothers. Jonathan and Simon Maccabee still lived to carry on the struggle for independence.

Jewish ritual objects, including two seven-branched candlesticks, are shown on the base of a gold goblet of the 2nd century C.E. found in a Jewish catacomb in Rome, where it was hidden from the Romans. The objects shown on the goblet are believed to have been taken from the Temple in Jerusalem when it was desecrated by Antiochus IV of Syria.

The word *menorah* refers specifically to the huge seven-branched golden candle-holder that stood in the Temple of Jerusalem. It was removed by the Romans when they destroyed Jerusalem in 70 C.E. This bronze 4th century menorah was found in Egypt.

The Torah (Exodus 25:31–40) provides the construction details of the Temple menorah. It was made by Bezalel and hammered out of a solid slab of gold. According to the Torah it stood seven feet tall, weighed 100 pounds, and was seven-branched.

The Great Assembly

Meantime, the Seleucid state was torn apart by inner confusion and strife. King Antiochus had died and the Syrian nobles were fighting each other over the right to the throne. Each contender, hoping to gain Judean support, sent an envoy to Jonathan with messages of friendship, gifts, and promises of peace.

Simon Rules Judea / 145–134 B.C.E.

Simon, the last of the Maccabean brothers, succeeded Jonathan as high priest. He expelled the last remaining Syrian soldiers from the country. Garrison by garrison, the Syrians were forced to abandon their strongholds. At last Judea was free from the Syrian yoke.

Independence at Last

For the first time in centuries, Judea was no longer ruled by foreigners. The people rejoiced. Simon convened the Great Assembly, a representative body of priests and other communal leaders. This body, which is also known as the Sanhedrin, proclaimed Simon and his descendants high priests and rulers of Judea.

Simon's reign brought happiness and prosperity to Judea. Jews came from Babylonia, Egypt, and many distant lands to visit Jerusalem and the Temple. Traders came once again with their wares and greatly increased Judea's commerce.

Like his brother Judah, Simon realized that Rome was a power to be reckoned with. As Judah had done before him, Simon sent a delegation to Rome to negotiate a pact renewing the alliance between the two states.

John Hyrcanus Seeks Conquest

When Simon died in 134 B.C.E., he was succeeded by his son, John Hyrcanus. An ambitious man, Hyrcanus wanted to extend the borders of Judea by conquering other lands. Taking advantage of the confusion that prevailed in Syria, John Hyrcanus began by capturing Gaza and other coastal cities. His troops went on to conquer Idumea (Edom) and Nabatea in the area that is today Jordan.

Hyrcanus struck new coins to commemorate his reign. Under his rule, Judea grew prosperous and expanded its borders. But many people were dissatisfied with his policies.

A temple in the rock-cut city of Petra, the capital of Nabatea. John Hyrcanus expanded the borders of Israel and conquered Idumea and Nabatea, in Jordan.

Pharisees and Sadducees

As a result of the discontent with John Hyrcanus, two opposing parties developed in Judea, the Pharisees and the Sadducees.

The Sadducees were named after Zadok, the high priest of Solomon's time. Most of them were high-ranking priests, noblemen, and wealthy merchants. They supported John Hyrcanus and his stern, literal interpretation of the Torah, which often worked for the benefit of the upper classes.

They were opposed by the Pharisees, who took their name from the Hebrew word *perushim* ("separatists"). The Pharisees favored a more democratic approach and were concerned about the welfare of the common people; they advocated a more flexible interpretation of the Torah.

All the Hasmoneans until now had ruled Judea as high priests and hereditary princes. After the death of John Hyrcanus in 105 B.C.E., his son Aristobulus declared himself king. But Aristobulus died after ruling for one year. He was succeeded by his brother Alexander Jannai. Like John Hyrcanus, Jannai was a worldly man.

The aristocratic Sadducees gave Jannai their full support. During his 27-year reign, Judea was involved in many military campaigns.

The struggle between Pharisees and Sadducees grew very bitter during this time. With the help of Alexander Jannai, the Sadducees obtained a majority in the Great Assembly, Judea's supreme court.

The Oral Tradition

The Pharisees and Sadducees disagreed about the Oral Tradition. More interpretations were needed, and added, to meet the requirements of changing political, economical, and social conditions.

The Pharisees regarded the Oral Tradition as having equal status with the written Torah. The Sadducees did not. As a result, there were many differences between them in practice, holiday, and theology. The Pharisees believed that knowledge of the Torah should be spread throughout the populace, whereas the Sadducees felt that it was unnecessary for the people to understand all aspects of the Torah. They held that knowledge of the Torah should be reserved for the priests. Most of the people of Judea sided with the Pharisees.

The Majority Party

When Alexander Jannai grew old, he realized that the Pharisees had become a strong force. He advised his wife and successor, Salome Alexandra, to grant them a more active part in the government. Accordingly, Queen Salome appointed a Pharisee, her brother Simon ben Shetah, as the new president of the Sanhedrin (Great Assembly). The choice was a wise one, for Simon ben Shetah was a learned, able man who instituted many good laws.

An Era of Peace / ca. 76–67 B.C.E.

Queen Salome's reign was an era of peace. She established a fairer balance between the two parties in the Sanhedrin.

Pleased by this separation of state and priesthood, the Pharisees loyally supported the queen. They were now the majority They saw to it that only responsible men, familiar with Jewish law, were appointed as judges. Guided by Simon ben Shetah, the Pharisees improved the Judean school system. During the seven years of Salome Alexandra's reign, Judea prospered and flourished.

Civil War in Judea

After Salome's death in 67 B.C.E. her two sons, Aristobulus II and Hyrcanus II, contended for the crown. Jew fought Jew in a bitter civil war which lasted for five years. Finally, the warring factions turned to Rome to arbitrate their dispute. The Roman general Pompey had just taken Damascus. To this great general came three separate Judean delegations seeking protection and help. One group represented Hyrcanus, another represented Aristobulus, and the third, a delegation of Pharisees, represented the Judean people.

Bust of Julius Caesar.

Roman Legions Overrun Judea / 63 B.C.E.

The Pharisees asked Pompey to choose neither of the sons of Salome but to restore rule by the high priest, who would be aided by the Sanhedrin. Pompey, thinking first of what would be best for Rome, decided in favor of Hyrcanus, the weaker contender. Soon afterward Pompey's legions overran Judea, capturing Jerusalem after a three-month siege. Thousands of Jews lost their lives and many others were enslaved. Aristobulus was carried off to Rome along with scores of other Jewish captives.

After almost 80 years of independence, Judea was once again under the domination of a foreign power. The Judean coastal cities and Mediterranean ports now became part of the Roman province of Syria.

Under Roman rule Judea was divided into five districts, and Hyrcanus was left to govern only Jerusalem itself and the immediately surrounding area. Meanwhile, a bitter struggle broke out between Pompey and Julius Caesar for control of the Roman Empire. Caesar marched against Pompey and defeated him. Pompey fled to Egypt, where he was murdered by his own men in 48 B.C.E.

This 15th century French painting shows Pompey and his soldiers desecrating and looting the Holy Temple.

Julius Caesar and the Jews

Hyrcanus II Supports Caesar

Although Pompey was gone, Caesar still faced opposition in Rome. In Judea he won the support of Hyrcanus II and his chief advisor, Antipater. The latter was a clever, scheming man from Idumea whose parents had been converted to Judaism.

A Jewish army of 3,000 men fought alongside Caesar's legions during the campaign in Egypt in which he defeated Ptolemy XII, the husband of Cleopatra. In gratitude for the help the Jews had given him, Caesar reinstated Hyrcanus II as high priest and appointed him ethnarch (secular ruler) of Judea. Caesar rewarded Antipater with the high honor of Roman citizenship.

In addition, he reinstated the rights of the Jewish community of Alexandria, which had been taken away some years earlier by a hostile government.

Antipater Becomes Procurator

In 47 B.C.E., Caesar appointed Antipater procurator (governor) of Judea. Since most Judeans resented Antipater as an outsider because he was an Idumean and the son of converts, this caused great dissatisfaction. Antipater, in turn, appointed his older son, Phasael, as governor of Jerusalem. The governorship of Galilee he gave to his brilliant but ruthlessly ambitious younger son, Herod.

This is the well-preserved amphitheater in Caesarea. It was built by King Herod for the Roman procurators.

The Romans were brilliant engineers and prolific builders. They left their imprint on the civilizations of the countries they conquered. Many Roman roads, monuments, aqueducts, and amphitheaters have survived the ravages of time and war.
This is one of the high-level aqueducts built by the Romans in Caesarea. It brought water from the local spring to the city.

Herod the Cruel Becomes Ruler / ca. 37–4 B.C.E.

Under the leadership of a man named Hezekiah, a band of rebels was organized in Galilee to fight for Jewish independence from Rome. When Herod learned about their activities, he had the entire group arrested and executed.

The news of Herod's cruelty shocked the Sanhedrin. Herod was summoned to stand trial. Accused men usually came before the Great Assembly dressed in black as a sign of humility. Herod, however, entered the court dressed in the purple garments of a prince and escorted by soldiers.

The members of the Sanhedrin wanted to punish Herod, but they had to be lenient because he was under the protection of Hyrcanus, the high priest.

In 44 B.C.E. Julius Caesar was assassinated by his political opponents. This had unfortunate consequences for Judea. Caesar had been its protector, but Mark Antony, the ruler of Rome's eastern territories, was a friend of Herod. Jewish delegations repeatedly went to see him to complain about Herod's cruelty, but Antony ignored them.

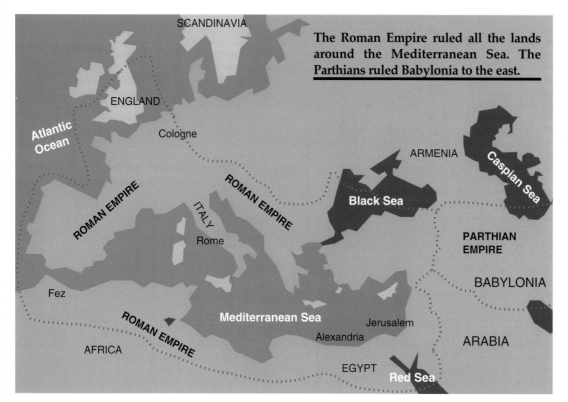

The Roman Empire ruled all the lands around the Mediterranean Sea. The Parthians ruled Babylonia to the east.

SCANDINAVIA

ENGLAND

Atlantic Ocean

Cologne

ARMENIA

Caspian Sea

Black Sea

ROMAN EMPIRE

ROMAN EMPIRE

ITALY

Rome

PARTHIAN EMPIRE

BABYLONIA

Fez

Mediterranean Sea

Jerusalem

Alexandria

ARABIA

ROMAN EMPIRE

AFRICA

EGYPT

Red Sea

King Herod built the city of Caesarea as a seat of government for the Roman procurators. He named it in honor of Caesar Augustus. All that now remains of this once busy deepwater port are fragmented stone pillars awash in the Mediterranean Sea.

Instead, he made Herod and his brother Phasael tetrarchs, or co-rulers, of Judea and executed the members of the Jewish delegations.

Antigonus Overthrows Herod / ca. 47 B.C.E.

In 40 B.C.E. the Parthians, an Iranian people who now ruled the former Seleucid territories in Persia and Mesopotamia, invaded Palestine. Taking advantage of the situation, Antigonus, a grandson of Alexander Jannai and Hyrcanus' nephew gathered all the discontented groups under his leadership and joined forces with the invaders. For about three years, Antigonus ruled as king of Judea, and he remained in power after Rome drove back the Parthians. The politically shrewd Herod,

Portrait coin of Mark Antony, 41 B.C.E.

Herod's Reign of Terror / ca. 37–4 B.C.E.

With the help of Roman legions, Herod entered Judea, his new kingdom. He laid siege to Jerusalem, and after five months of fighting, the city surrendered. Herod immediately executed the leaders of the opposition. Antigonus, too, was executed.

Herod proved to be a cruel ruler. He was very ambitious, and craved splendor and fame. Deeply suspicious, he saw signs of rebellion and danger everywhere. Many people had to pay with their lives because of his fears.

Constantly fearing that a member of the Hasmonean family would take the throne from him, Herod sought to make his position secure by a reign of terror and murder. He executed two prominent Hasmoneans, Hyrcanus, who had returned from Parthian captivity a broken old man, and his own wife, Mariamne, as well as their two sons.

Memorial inscription of the Roman 10th Legion, which was stationed at Jerusalem after the city was conquered by Titus in 70 C.E.

however, sailed for Rome. Combining bribes and personal charm, he persuaded Mark Antony and Octavian, the co-rulers of the Roman Empire, that only he could keep the Jews under control. He returned home as king of Judea. Technically Judea was again an independent state, but for practical purposes it was a Roman dependency.

Herod's family tomb in Jerusalem. Here the monarch buried his wife Mariamne and his two sons after murdering them in a maniacal rage.

Economic Prosperity

Herod the Great

Despite his cruelty, history refers to Herod as Herod the Great. While the Judeans hated and feared him, the Romans admired him as a loyal ally and efficient administrator and for keeping the peace. In addition, he implemented policies to increase Judea's trade and prosperity.

Situated between Syria and Egypt, Judea was crossed by the great trade routes that ran east and west. Caravans from Arabia and Persia with goods for the west made their first stop in Judea. Traders even came from distant India. And ships from Greece and Africa landed at Judea's Mediterranean ports.

Herod gained control of several free cities on the Judean coast which had been built by Greek and Roman settlers. These cities had been part of a confederation called the Decapolis, or "League of Ten Cities." As part of Judea, they brought new wealth to the country.

Herod collected high taxes from his people. Some of the money went to Rome, and some paid for his own Judean projects.

Herod the Builder

Herod delighted in building elaborate structures and founded two new cities named in honor of his Roman friends: Tiberias, in honor of the emperor Tiberius; and the coastal city of Caesarea, in honor of Caesar Augustus. He also built amphitheaters and arenas, where gladiators and captives had to fight and wrestle with untamed beasts, as was the custom in the arenas of Rome.

The Temple / ca. 20 B.C.E.

Unquestionably, Herod's most ambitious project was the improvement and enlargement of the Temple. For 500 years the

The Herodium fortress, near Bethlehem. It is situated on a mountaintop and is highly defensible. The fortress also served as a palace. After the Great Revolt in 70 C.E., it provided a refuge for rebels who managed to escape from Jerusalem.

Temple built by the returning Babylonian exiles had served as the nation's sanctuary. In no way like the splendid Temple of Solomon's reign, it was a small, simple building, and was deteriorating with age. Herod spared no cost or effort in rebuilding the Temple. Portion by portion, his workmen and architects restored and improved it. Throughout his reign, Herod continued work on the Temple compound. The project was begun in 20 B.C.E. and was not finished until several years after Herod's death.

Herod's Temple was a magnificent structure. Throughout Asia Minor people marveled at its beauty and splendor. Like all of Herod's buildings, it was built in the classic Greek style. Herod raised a strong wall around the Temple compound, and above the main gate he placed an eagle, the golden emblem of Rome.

This deeply offended the people. How could a warlike emblem be allowed to disgrace God's peaceful sanctuary? Thus, while the beauty of Herod's Temple gave him prestige abroad, it did not win him the love of his people.

Masada, the Fortress

The ruins of the synagogue on Masada. The round pillars in the center of the photograph supported the synagogue's roof.

The fortress of Masada was built by King Herod. It has been excavated and a large part has been reconstructed.

Masada

To guarantee internal security and protect the borders of his kingdom, Herod built a number of fortresses, including Antonia in Jerusalem, Herodium near Bethlehem, and Masada near the Dead Sea.

Masada is situated on a high rock in the Judean desert. The cliffs that surround it are steep and make the fortress easy to defend.

One of Herod's first projects on Masada was the creation of a system to ensure an adequate supply of water. He built a series of cisterns which stored rain water for use during the dry season. Almost the entire summit was enclosed with a thick fortified wall, with 30 watchtowers and four gates.

Herod constructed several palaces at Masada, containing many rooms, bathrooms, and a cold-water pool paved with mosaics. In addition, there were a series of storehouses where oil, flour, wine, and foods were kept in special jars. Other storehouses contained munitions and weapons.

Two mikvot (ritual baths) and a synagogue have also been uncovered on Masada.

Masada was the last Zealot stronghold during the Jewish war against Rome in 66–72 C.E.

The Leaders of Judea

The Sanhedrin

Distrusting Herod because he was an Idumean, and distrusting the high priests because they were now appointed either by Herod or by the Roman government, the people of Judea turned for leadership to the religious teachers and scholars who made up the Great Assembly, or Sanhedrin.

Students and scholars from the Jewish communities of Egypt and Babylonia, Syria and Persia, North Africa and Rome, came to Jerusalem, the center of Jewish learning, to learn Torah from them.

The Chain of Tradition

The Sanhedrin was the institution where the laws of the Torah were expounded, interpreted, and codified in accordance with the Oral Tradition.

According to tractate Avot of the Mishnah, the chain of tradition started with Moses. He handed it on to Joshua, who in turn passed it on to the elders. From them it came down to the prophets, who handed it over to the Men of the Great Assembly. The latter, sometimes referred to as scribes, were the true spiritual leaders of Judea and world Jewry.

How the Sanhedrin Functioned

The Great Sanhedrin had 71 members, most of whom were Pharisees. It was presided over by two leaders, known as *zugot* ("pairs") One of the zugot was the *nasi* ("prince" or "chief"); the other was the *av bet din* ("presiding judge").

The most famous of these "pairs" of scholars were Hillel and Shammai. The discussions in the Sanhedrin were often sharp and brilliant, and many of the debates and legal decisions of the zugot became famous.

The stone *cathedra* (chair) of Moses from the 3rd century synagogue at Korazim, in Galilee. Chairs of this kind were installed in ancient synagogues for the principal teacher of the law, or for a person the community wished to honor.

Hillel / 1st cent. B.C.E.

Hillel was a brilliant young man who came to Judea from Babylonia. Although very poor, he loved learning. He earned the money to pay for admission to the lectures at the academy by cutting wood.

One cold winter's night when he did not have the admission fee, Hillel lay atop the roof of the schoolhouse and listened to the lectures until he fell asleep from exhaustion. The next morning, when the academy assembled, the scholars found the hall

These catacombs are called the Tomb of the Sanhedrin. Inside are a large number of burial chambers carved into the rock. It is the traditional place where the members of the Sanhedrin were buried. The tomb is in Jerusalem.

exceptionally dark. Looking up at the sky-light, they saw Hillel's body blocking the sun. Touched by the young man's great devotion to learning, the teachers provided him with a scholarship.

Hillel became a renowned sage. He returned to Babylonia to teach, but was invited back to Jerusalem to join the Great Sanhedrin. His wisdom and learning were recognized by Jewish scholars everywhere.

Once Hillel was asked to tell what he considered the fundamental principle of Judaism. His famous answer was: "What is hateful to you, do not do unto others. All the rest of the Torah is merely an explanation of this rule." Hillel said that the way to the Torah, and to God, was to love peace and love mankind. He valued the unity of Israel above all, and warned his students never to set themselves apart from the community of the Jewish people.

So greatly respected was Hillel that the office of nasi of the Sanhedrin became hereditary in his family. He became the founder of the school of Torah interpretation known as Bet Hillel ("House of Hillel").

Shammai / 1st cent. B.C.E.

Hillel's colleague Shammai, the av bet din, was a brilliant scholar who came from one of Jerusalem's wealthy, noble families. Stern and conservative, he often differed on questions of law with Hillel. While Hillel usually took the more lenient, flexible view, Shammai interpreted the law strictly. He was a pious scholar, devoted to preserving the Torah and the Jewish way of life.

The famous debates between Hillel and Shammai caused a great stir in the Jewish communities of their day. Wherever Jews

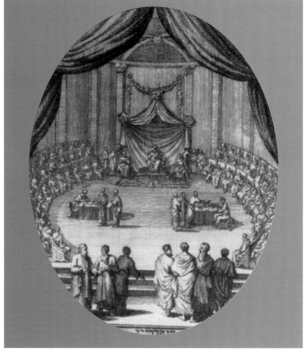

An engraving in a Hebrew-Latin edition of the Mishnah (1744). It illustrates a session of the Sanhedrin.

assembled, studied, and prayed, the teachings of Hillel and Shammai were discussed.

An oil press from talmudic times. Ripe olives were crushed and olive oil was extracted. Olive oil was a basic food in ancient Israel.

Revolt in Judea / ca. –14 CE

Under Roman Rule

Herod died in 4 B.C.E. Soon afterward, Augustus, the Roman emperor, divided his kingdom among his three sons, making each of them an ethnarch. Judea, Samaria, and Idumea were now Roman possessions ruled by officials called procurators. The procurators were cruel and ruthless. They collected high taxes, taking a good portion for themselves before sending the rest to Rome. Garrisons of Roman soldiers were stationed throughout the land.

Although Rome seemed all-powerful, the people never gave up the hope of regaining their independence. In the hills of Galilee, guerilla fighters rallied to Judah, the son of Hezekiah, the leader executed by Herod.

The Pharisees Oppose Rebellion

The Pharisees and the Great Sanhedrin in Jerusalem opposed this uprising. They advocated passive resistance and steadfast devotion to Jewish law. Like the earlier revolts against Assyria and Babylon, they warned, open rebellion against Rome would end in utter destruction.

The Zealots Form a Party

Violently opposed to the pacifism of the Pharisees, the rebels founded their own party, calling themselves Zealots. Many of the more extreme Zealots formed partisan bands in the Galilean hills. They ambushed Roman transports and attacked Roman patrols.

This was a terrible time for the people of Judea. Those who were suspected of anti-Roman activities were tortured in Roman prisons. Many others were executed by crucifixion.

The Essenes

More and more people began to yearn for the coming of the Messiah, a savior whom God would send to defeat their enemies and institute a golden age of peace, prosperity, and piety in an independent Jewish state. Some formed groups or sects which adopted a pious lifestyle designed to prepare them for the Messianic era and perhaps even to bring it closer.

The Essenes were the best-known of these sects. They were dedicated to a life of purity, study, and charity. They owned no property as individuals, but held everything in common. Most of them lived together in secluded communities, following their own strict rules. They were extreme pacifists, totally opposed to war and bloodshed. They ate no meat and lived frugally. Many of them went out into the desert for long periods of fasting, meditation, and prayer.

The famous Dead Sea Scrolls, which were discovered in a cave near Qumran, are a rich source of information about the beliefs and rituals of the Jewish sects of this period.

The Dead Sea Scrolls are the oldest Hebrew manuscripts in existence. They are housed in the Shrine of the Book, in the Israel Museum, Jerusalem. The scroll of Isaiah is displayed fully opened around a drum.

Birth of Christianity

John the Baptist / 1st cent. C.E.
Around this time a wandering preacher named Yohanan, known in history as John the Baptist, made his appearance. John spoke of the coming of the Messiah, called for repentance, and bathed his followers in the waters of the Jordan River as a symbolic act of purification. This act, which resembled the ritual bath of the Essenes, is now known as baptism.

Before long Herod Antipas, the tetrarch of Galilee, learned about John's activities. Fearing that John's sermons would stir the people to revolt, he had him arrested and executed.

Jesus of Nazareth / ca. 29 C.E.
Among those influenced by John's sermons and baptized by him was a young man from Nazareth named Joshua, known to history as Jesus. He too traveled through the land with a band of disciples, preaching to the people.

Jesus was familiar with the teachings of the great sages and frequently quoted them. But his own teachings differed from those of the Pharisees. Whereas the Pharisee scholars based their opinions on the Oral Tradition, Jesus often spoke in his

The remains of the synagogue at Capernaum on the shores of the Sea of Galilee.

own name and challenged the accepted religious and political authorities.

Pontius Pilate Crucifies Jesus
In the year 29 C.E., at the time of Passover, Jesus went to Jerusalem. During festivals, when the city was crowded with pilgrims, Jerusalem was a hotbed of revolt. Amid the tumult in the crowded streets, Jesus' disciples proclaimed that he was the Messiah. From the Roman standpoint this was a serious matter. It meant that he might try to overthrow their government.

Roman soldiers arrested Jesus and brought him to the procurator, Pontius Pilate. Accused of rabble-rousing and of pretending to be the "King of the Jews," Jesus was condemned to death by crucifixion.

The Followers of Jesus
The followers of Jesus remained together after his death. Many of them believed that he had risen from the grave and would return in glory as the Messiah. Within a few years, from this small group, emerged the new religion of Christianity.

The limestone rock, excavated in Caesarea, is inscribed with a dedication to Pontius Pilate, the Roman governor who authorized the crucifixion of Jesus.

The Zealots Resist

The Zealots were Jewish patriots. They hated Rome and all it stood for. They considered everyone who collaborated with the Romans to be an enemy. Seeing themselves as successors of the Hasidim and the valiant Maccabees, they conducted a guerrilla war against Rome and its supporters.

The Zealots were a serious problem for the Roman government. Many members of the Great Sanhedrin, feeling that it was important to keep the peace, also opposed them. The Jewish people were not united and often disagreed about which policy to follow.

Rebellion Against Florus / 64–66 C.E.

Florus was the last Roman procurator of Judea. When he came to Judea, he took no interest in the problems of the Jews. He increased taxes, which were already high. He even seized a great sum of gold from the Temple treasury.

The Jews were indignant. The Temple funds had been raised by voluntary contributions and were intended for charitable purposes, not to build up the Roman treasury.

An Independent Jerusalem

The people of Jerusalem, led by the Zealots, armed themselves and rose up against the Romans. Men, women, and children joined in the fighting. The Roman garrison, unable to put down the rebellion or to hold the city, was forced to retreat.

Soon another Roman army appeared before Jerusalem, but it was ambushed and

This ancient block of stone was a part of the wall of a building in the Temple compound in Jerusalem. The Hebrew inscription reads, "To the place of trumpeting."

The Essenes were a religious sect in Palestine at the end of the Second Temple period. They lived a severe, mystic life in isolated monastic communities. Each member of the sect worked and contributed manual labor for the benefit of the group. They believed in personal and ritual purity.

The Roman army marched through Palestine, destroying Jewish cities and strong points. They leveled the Essene settlement at Qumran.

Most scholars attribute the Dead Sea Scrolls to the Essenes. Excavations at Qumran have enabled archaeologists to reconstruct their lives.

defeated. Many of its weapons fell into Jewish hands. Thus, in the fall of 66 C.E., Judea began its last brief period of independence. Once more the Jews ruled themselves.

The Romans Attack / 67 C.E.

The people were overjoyed, even though they knew that Rome would not give up easily. They were ready to fight to preserve their freedom.

In the spring of 67 C.E., a Roman army of 60,000 well-equipped soldiers commanded by Vespasian, the greatest general of the day, invaded Galilee. Vespasian was aided by his son, the able young general Titus, who brought reinforcements from Egypt. One by one, the Jewish strongpoints in Galilee fell. Led by Yohanan (John) of Giscala, the few remaining Jewish fighters fled to Jerusalem.

Revolt in Rome / 66 C.E.

While Vespasian was preparing to besiege Jerusalem, he received news of a revolt in Rome. The emperor Nero had committed suicide, and three contenders, one after another, had seized the throne. All three had been murdered within a year, and the Roman army had proclaimed Vespasian as the new emperor. Leaving his troops under the command of Titus, Vespasian left for Rome to take control of the government.

For five centuries, Rome dominated the ancient world. Among its conquests were Spain, France, England, Greece and the Balkans, Mesopotamia, Armenia, Egypt, Judea, and North Africa. At its height the Roman Empire controlled an expanse which included 100 million people.

The Roman armies were well equipped and led by talented commanders. Success in battle came easily to this well-disciplined fighting machine.

These Roman soldiers belonged to the Praetorian Guard, the emperor's personal bodyguard

The ancient city of Gamla is located in the Golan. It is called Gamla, because it is situated on a hill that is shaped like a camel (Gamla). During the war against Rome it was besieged and captured by Vespasian, and after a month of severe fighting.

In revenge for their loses, the Romans massacred all the inhabitants. The above are the ruins of the synagogue in Gamla.

Portrait coin of Vespasian, 69-79 C.E.

Judea Is Defeated / 70 C.E.

Jerusalem Under Siege

In the year 70 C.E., Titus began the siege of Jerusalem. It went on for several months. In the final hours of their resistance, the defenders of Jerusalem were united. Despite hunger and hardship, they held out courageously. Day and night they heard the heavy thud of Roman battering rams and the terrifying ballistas, which shot 100-pound boulders into the city. The outer walls of Jerusalem gave way; so did the third, northern wall. Many still hoped that some miracle would happen and the city would be saved.

On the 17th of Tammuz, conditions in Jerusalem grew worse. The fighting in the Temple area was so heavy that for the first time since the days of Judah Maccabee, the sacrifices had to be discontinued. Yet the defenders fought on. Their leaders, Yohanan of Giscala and Simon Bar Giora, gave them courage.

Josephus as Historian / ca. 38–ca. 100 C.E.

Outside the walls, Titus spurred his soldiers on to make an end to the bloody siege. Titus had a strange companion in those days, Josephus Flavius, a descendant of the Maccabees whose Hebrew name was Joseph ben Mattiyahu ha-Kohen. From the enemy camp, Josephus watched the defeat of his people.

At the age of 26, Josephus had been was sent on a diplomatic mission to Rome, where he remained for two years at the court of Nero. On his return in 65 C.E. he found Judea in revolt against the Romans. Despite Zealot suspicions of his loyalty, he was given command of the Jewish forces in Galilee. In 67 C.E., when his troops were defeated by Vespasian's army, Josephus saved his life by surrendering. During the

The Arch of Titus in Rome.

siege of Jerusalem, he helped Titus by trying to demoralize the city's defenders. After the city's fall, he was rewarded for his treachery and took a Roman name.

Josephus wrote several books which serve as our main source of information about the very important period of Jewish history in which he lived.

The Temple Is Destroyed / 70 C.E.

On the 9th of Av in the year 70 C.E., on the anniversary of the day Nebuchadnezzar had destroyed the Temple of Solomon, Titus stormed the Temple area. A Roman soldier climbed the wall and hurled a burning torch. In moments, the Temple was in flames. Some of the fighters tried to escape,

This Roman coin, inscribed *Judaea Capta,* "Judea is captured," recalls the Roman victory in the first Jewish revolt.

to make a stand in another Judean fortress. But they did not succeed. Yohanan of Giscala and Simon Bar Giora, with many of their brave men, were taken captive.

The Arch of Triumph

When Titus returned to Rome, the Jewish captives were paraded in front of the populace. They were forced to march in a procession into the Roman Forum, carrying the treasures that Titus had taken from Judea.

The Romans customarily erected an arch of triumph whenever a victorious general returned from a military campaign. The Arch of Titus, commemorating the defeat of Judea, can still be seen in Rome. One of the reliefs on the arch shows the Jewish captives marching in Titus' triumphal procession.

The Destruction of Judea / 70 C.E.

Judea was destroyed and its people conquered. More than a million people died in the war, and thousands were carried off into exile and slavery. The Jews lost their independence. Palestine was again governed by a representative of the Roman emperor.

Jewish communities throughout the world mourned for Judea, for Jerusalem, and above all for the Temple, which had been the spiritual center of their lives.

Judea was a land of desolation. Nothing of the Temple was left except the ruins of its western wall. Year by year, Jews assembled there in prayer, conducting services, reading from the Torah. Many wept as they stood by the ruined wall. On the 9th of Av, the anniversary of the destruction, Jewish pilgrims would come from many lands to mourn for the lost Temple.

A copy of the carving on the Arch of Titus, showing the Menorah and other furniture of the Temple being carried in triumph through the streets of Rome.

Despite the loss of their land and their Temple, the Jews continued to live in accordance with the laws of the Torah. It gave them hope and courage to face the future.

After the revolt Josephus wrote *The Jewish War*. In it he graphically describes the heroism of the Jewish soldiers. This 11th century drawing is from the Latin version of *The Jewish War*. Joseph, wearing a crown and seated on a throne, is presenting his book to Vespasian.

The Fall of Masada / 73 C.E.

The Romans had captured Jerusalem in 70 C.E., but some Jewish soldiers refused to give up. These valiant resistance fighters took refuge in Masada, Herod's palace-fortress on a flat-topped rock plateau in the desolate Judean desert, overlooking the Dead Sea. Although the Temple had been destroyed and Jerusalem had fallen, they stood their ground. For seven months, the Romans battled against the last Jewish stronghold. Finally, they managed to breach the wall of Masada and were poised to storm the fortress in overwhelming strength.

On the first day of Passover in 72 C.E. the Jewish leader, Eleazar ben Yair, called together all his soldiers. He advised them to take their own lives rather than be taken prisoner.

During Roman victory celebrations, thousands of prisoners, many of them Jews, were thrown into the arena and died battling wild, hungry beasts. The Jews atop Masada did not wish to become slaves and participate in the deadly spectacles in the Roman arenas.

Catapults of various sizes were used to hurl large stones into enemy lines. The silently falling stones from above instilled fear in the hearts of the enemy. They were also used in teams of batteries to rain death on the exposed enemy. The heavy stones could easily kill or maim a combatant.

Roman battering ram.

The Jewish defenders who faced the might of Rome were poorly armed. On the other hand, the Romans were equipped with the most modern armaments of the period. Roman catapults could hurl heavy boulders with great force. The Romans also employed battering rams, which destroyed defense walls and paved the way for the Roman infantry.

"We know in advance that tomorrow we shall fall into the enemy's hands," he said, "but we still have the free choice of dying a noble death together with our loved ones. Let our wives die undisgraced, and our children free from the shackles of slavery!"

Eleazar ben Yair's soldiers agreed. When the Romans entered the fortress the next day, their victory was an empty one.

In *The Jewish War*, Josephus records their astonishment at what they found.

"The Romans, expecting further resistance, were under arms at daybreak and advanced to the assault. Not a single defender was to be seen. On all sides there was an awesome silence. They were at a loss to guess what had happened. At last they called out to any one within. Their shouts were heard by the old women, who emerged from the caverns and informed the Romans of the deed and how it was done. When they came upon the rows of the dead, the Roman enemies admired the

nobility and utter contempt for death displayed by so many.

"Masada being thus taken, the Roman general left a garrison on the spot and departed. For not an enemy of Rome remained throughout the country, the whole having now been subdued by this protracted war."

A clay fragment with the name "Yair" found atop Masada. It may refer to the Jewish leader Eliazar ben Yair.

During the revolt against Rome, the rebels minted bronze and silver coins. The inscriptions read: "Freedom of Jerusalem" or "For the Redemption of Zion." Coins such as this one were found in Masada.

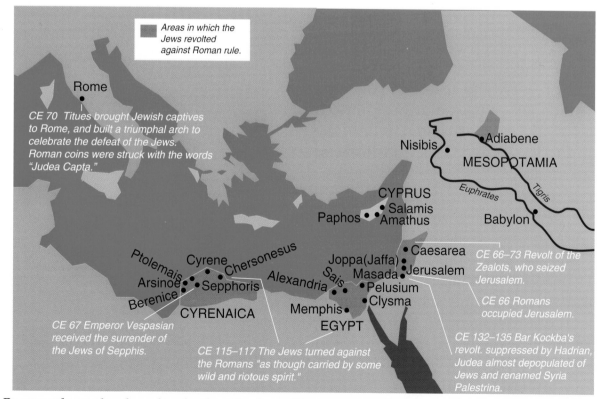

Roman rule was harsh, and under the rule of cruel Roman procurators, law and order broke down. Riots flared up all over Israel, and Roman troops were frequently attacked by bands of Jewish rebels.

The Struggle for Survival / 1st century C.E.

In the days before the siege of Jerusalem, many felt that Rome was sure to win. They feared that the Jews would not survive as a people if the Romans destroyed their country.

But there were others who believed that the Jews did not need a land or a Temple to be united. They felt that the Torah was a sufficiently strong bond. Among those who held this view was Rabban Yohanan ben Zakkai, a scholar who had been a member of the Great Sanhedrin and now became one of the great leaders of Jewish history.

Josephus before Emperor Vespasian, from a 12th century manuscript.

A Plan for Survival

Yohanan ben Zakkai knew that Judaism would survive if the Torah lived on in the hearts of the people. Like most of the Pharisees, he had opposed the war with Rome. Hating bloodshed, he believed in passive resistance. He had taught that true dignity would come not from rebellion but from faithful observance of the Torah

When the Romans prepared to lay siege to Jerusalem, Yohanan ben Zakkai thought of a way to preserve the Torah. He decided to start a school—an academy of Jewish learning—away from Jerusalem, where the Torah could be studied and questions of Jewish law discussed.

In those days it was impossible to leave Jerusalem. With the city preparing for the Roman attack, the Zealots were on the lookout for traitors. Many people were falsely accused of treason.

Determined to start his school. Yohanan had himself put into a coffin. His disciples, pretending he was dead, carried him out of Jerusalem under the watchful eyes of the Zealots, presumably to bury him.

Once they were outside the city, Yohanan ben Zakkai emerged from the coffin, very much alive. Before long he and his companions were stopped by a Roman patrol. Yohanan asked to be brought before their commander, Vespasian.

Portrait coin of Vespasian (69–79 C.E.)

Vespasian and Yohanan

The Roman general granted the scholar an audience, for he knew that Yohanan had opposed the war. Yohanan told Vespasian that he would soon become emperor of Rome. Very pleased by this prediction, Vespasian promised to grant anything Yohanan might request. This was exactly what Yohanan ben Zakkai had hoped for. He promptly asked for permission to set up a school in Yavneh, a small town on the seacoast. Vespasian agreed.

The School at Yavneh

Yohanan ben Zakkai at once set up a school in Yavneh. There the scholars continued their studies and conducted services in the synagogue. Eventually, Yohanan formed a Sanhedrin modeled after the Great Sanhedrin of Jerusalem, a court of 71 scholars who decided on all questions of law and learning, and on the proper interpretation of the Torah.

When the news came that Jerusalem had fallen and the Temple had been destroyed, Yohanan wept and tore his clothes in mourning. Yet he did not allow his disciples to despair.

Yohanan ben Zakkai

Rabban Yohanan ben Zakkai was the first nasi, or president, of the Sanhedrin in Yavneh. He was beloved for his humility, his love and respect for everyone. Yohanan ben Zakkai realized that new judges, teachers, and scholars had to be trained and ordained, as had been the practice in the days of the Great Sanhedrin. These scholars would have the title of rabbi, which literally means "master." Once ordained, after completing the necessary studies, the rabbi would

cease to be a disciple and himself become a teacher. The rabbis educated at Yavneh would be links in the great, unbroken chain of teachers of the Torah.

Yohanan and those who followed him were called tannaim, meaning "repeaters" or "teachers." The period in which they were active is known as the tannaitic era. It ended around 200 C.E.

A Roman soldier with his combat equipment. The short sword was called a *gladium* and the shield was called a *scutum*.

The interior of the Yohanan ben Zakkai Sephardic synagogue in the Jewish Quarter of Old Jerusalem. It is one of the oldest synagogues in the Meah Shearim section of Jerusalem. In 1948 the synagogue was destroyed by the Arab Legion. It was rebuilt in 1972.

Christianity Begins / *ca. 65 CE*

Paul of Tarsus / ca. 65 C.E.

Some years after the death of Jesus of Nazareth, the sect that followed his teachings found a new leader in Paul of Tarsus. Paul, a Jew from what is now southern Turkey, had come to Jerusalem to study Torah. He opposed the Christians at first but then became a zealous adherent of the sect. Determined to spread the new creed, he traveled widely throughout the Diaspora, preaching to both Jews and non-Jews.

Paul regularly sent letters about the new religion's doctrines to the communities he had visited. Later these were gathered together with various other Christian writings, including the accounts of Jesus' life known as the Four Gospels, in a collection of books called the New Testament. The Christian Bible is made up of both the New Testament and the Hebrew Bible, which Christians refer to as the Old Testament.

The Christian Church

According to Christian tradition, Paul died in Rome during the persecution of the new religion that followed the great fire that consumed much of the city in 65 C.E. He left a major legacy, however. The small groups of converts he organized during his missionary journeys made new converts of their own and founded houses of worship which later became known as churches. Before long there were churches throughout the Roman Empire. They all felt themselves bound to one another in a single large community, the Christian Church.

Earliest known manuscript of the letters of Paul, 200 C.E.

A painting of Mark the author of one of the New Testament gospels. It is dated about 800 C.E.

Gamaliel II / late 1st century C.E.

Gamaliel Becomes Nasi

When Yohanan ben Zakkai retired as nasi of the Sanhedrin, his place was taken by Gamaliel II, a descendant of Hillel. Gamaliel applied all his energy to the task of preserving Judaism under the new conditions confronting the Jewish people.

Gamaliel was particularly concerned with devising ways for people to worship now that the Temple was destroyed and the local synagogues had to take its place. To this end he supervised the formulation of many new rituals and prayers, including prayers for the restoration of the Temple.

In addition, Gamaliel and his colleagues in Yavneh decided that portions from the Torah and the Prophets should be read in the synagogues every Sabbath and on the holidays. Shorter sections of the weekly Sabbath portions were to be read on Mondays and on Thursdays, when the farmers came to town to market their produce. Jews everywhere still follow this custom.

Since festival pilgrimages to Jerusalem were no longer possible, Gamaliel and the scholars also arranged the prayer services for Sukkot, Pesach, and Shavuot. They included readings about the rituals that had taken place in the Temple on these days.

Gamaliel was troubled by the bitter differences of opinion that often occurred in the Sanhedrin. Fearing that disputes would destroy its authority, he wanted the nasi to be the final arbitrator whenever the scholars differed. Many of the scholars angrily felt that Gamaliel was trying to make himself too powerful.

Gamaliel Is Dismissed and Reinstated

The opposition voted to remove Gamaliel from office. Gamaliel took his dismissal gracefully. He did not withdraw from the Sanhedrin but continued to attend its sessions, although his opinions were never shared by a majority. He also continued his teaching duties. Eventually, Gamaliel was reinstated as nasi of the Sanhedrin. But never again did he, or any other nasi, attempt to interfere with the Sanhedrin's democratic procedures.

Rabban Gamliel the Elder with three of his disciples, an illumination from the 13th century in the Sarajevo Haggadah.

Rabbi Akiva and the Mishnah / ca. 40–135 CE

Rabbi Akiva was the most outstanding of the many scholars and rabbis who taught at Yavneh. As a young man, Akiva had been an uneducated shepherd. He had married Rachel, the daughter of his wealthy master, and over the years she made many sacrifices to enable him to fulfill his ambition of learning Torah. Thanks to her efforts, he was able to attend the academy of Eliezer and Joshua, who were carrying on the work of Yohanan ben Zakkai. Akiva became the most brilliant scholar of the time. His decisions were concise and clear. He was not only a great scholar, but also a great teacher, and students eagerly flocked to his lectures at B'ne B'rak, where he founded his own academy.

The Mishnah of Rabbi Akiva

Rabbi Akiva initiated one of the most important projects in the history of Jewish law. With the aid of his colleagues, he set about systematically organizing the vast body of laws, discussions, and cases comprising the Oral Tradition. Akiva did not put all this down in writing, for it was not yet the custom to do so, but he originated the idea of classifying material by subject, arranging Sabbath laws, marriage laws, and laws of property as separate categories. Thanks to this system, which is now known as the Mishnah of Rabbi Akiva, scholars found it much easier to locate important information when researching questions of Jewish law and practice.

Rachel and Akiva

Not only did Rachel consent to Akiva's leaving her to attend the academy, but she even cut off her hair and sold it to a wig merchant in order to pay his tuition. Though she had no children at this time, and had to support herself,

she was willing to make the sacrifice to help her husband become a learned man.

Akiva stayed away 24 years. By the end of that time he had become the best student in the academy and was able to expound the Torah better than his teachers. He returned home as a great scholar attended by thousands of students.

The people crowded around to see the visiting scholar. Among them was an old man dressed in fine clothing but with a sorrowful appearance. "Many years ago," he said to the rabbi, "I made a vow. Now I am old and do not have many years left. I am sorry and would like to know if I can be released from my vow."

"What was the vow you made?" asked Rabbi Akiva.

"When my daughter enraged me by marrying a poor shepherd," said the man, "I swore I would never speak to her or help her in any way."

"Why did you make the vow?" asked Rabbi Akiva.

"Because he was an ignorant man who could not even read or write," said the old man.

"Vows cannot easily be broken," said Akiva, "but this one was made because of a certain condition. If the condition has changed, the vow need no longer be kept. You may consider your vow null and void, because I am that same ignorant shepherd."

Rachel's father was delighted to learn that his son-in-law was now a distinguished scholar. Weeping with joy, he embraced his long-lost daughter and his grandchildren. Respected leader and teacher of his people, Akiva never forgot to give credit to Rachel. When asked, "Who is really a rich man?" Akiva answered, "He who has a good wife."

Rabbi Akiva instructing his pupils. From the Sarajevo Haggadah.

A New Rebellion

Trajan's March of Conquest / 98–117 C.E.

Following the revolt, Judea went through a period of peace and reconstruction, but this changed when Trajan became the emperor of Rome in 98 C.E.. Filled with dreams of surpassing Alexander the Great's achievement, Trajan began a new march of conquest. His great ambition was to conquer far-off India. He began by invading Dacia (modern Romania) in 101 and 105 C.E., and in 113 he attacked the Parthian Empire.

Fragment of an ancient Torah scroll. It belongs to a Jewish family in the Israeli village of Peki'in in the Galilee. Peki'in has a record of Jewish settlement from the 1st century C.E. The inhabitants of this tiny agricultural village escaped Roman exile.

While Trajan was embroiled in these wars, rebellions broke out in many parts of the empire. The Jews of Cyprus, Egypt, and Cyrene revolted in 115–117, but the uprisings were cruelly suppressed. For the survivors, the only result was disappointment and hardship.

Hadrian Rebuilds Jerusalem / 117–138 C.E.

Trajan's campaign of conquest ended suddenly in 117 C.E. when he died on one of his expeditions. His successor, Hadrian, abandoned Trajan's policy of conquest. The Roman Empire was already huge and unwieldy, and Hadrian felt it was dangerous to add more territory. His legions were already hard-pressed putting down revolts in many areas—Germania, Gaul, and Britain; Spain, Egypt, Mesopotamia, Parthia, and Palestine. There was hardly a province that did not cause Hadrian worry.

Hadrian decided to rebuild Jerusalem. But how disappointed the Jews were when they realized what he had in mind! He was not building the Jerusalem of the past, the setting for the Temple of God. Instead, he was building a heathen city, with a circus and stadium, and with a temple for the gods of Rome. Hadrian visited the city and supervised the building projects himself. On the site of the Holy Temple he built an altar dedicated to the god Jupiter. At the same time he outlawed circumcision and issued other new laws that made it difficult to practice Judaism.

Engraved stone with the name of Emperor Trajan, found in Caesarea.

Bar Kochba's Revolt / *ca. 132–135 CE*

Judea had been at peace. The people had made no trouble even during the stormy days of Trajan's invasion of Parthia or when their fellow Jews in other countries revolted. But now the country seethed with anger and a rebellious spirit. Many Jews were impatient to rise against Rome and fight once more for freedom. The rebellious spirit spread even to the academy, where the scholars usually favored peace. Rabbi Akiva was one of the leaders of those who wanted to rise against Rome.

Son of a Star

By the time Hadrian came to Palestine in 129 C.E. to supervise the rebuilding of Jerusalem, Akiva was very old. Despite his advanced age, he still hoped to see his people living in freedom again. When he heard about Simon Bar Kozeba, a brave young man of great magnetism and religious fervor who was organizing a guerilla force to fight the Romans, Akiva felt that the time was at hand. He gave Bar Kozeba his support and renamed him Simon Bar Kochba ("Son of a Star"), a title that heralded his extraordinary strength and spirit. Like many others in this era of turmoil and expectation, Akiva came to believe that Bar Kochba might actually be the Messiah, sent by God to restore the political independence of the Jewish people.

Bust of Hadrian.

The Romans developed a wooden catapult that could throw giant stones very far. Because of its kicking action it was called an onager. An onager is a wild donkey which defends itself by kicking wildly.

The Revolt Begins / 132 C.E.

Hadrian's departure from Palestine was the signal for revolt. The insurrection began in 132 C.E. and lasted for three and a half years. Striking from secure hiding places in the caves and valleys, the Jewish fighters conducted lethal hit-and-run raids against the Romans. Everywhere, Roman outposts were attacked, Roman patrols were ambushed, and Roman supplies were taken. Revolt had broken out! Hadrian sent an army to reinforce the Palestine garrison, but his troops were defeated. Bar Kochba went from victory to victory, liberating one town after another, and the Roman army was chased into Syria.

A Period of Independence

Bar Kochba and his victorious army entered Jerusalem. Everyone rejoiced! They were free again, as in the days of the Maccabees. An altar was erected on the site of the Temple. An uncle of Bar Kochba, the priest Eleazar, officiated at the services. Bar Kochba was declared head of the state, to be assisted by Eleazar. Under the leadership of Bar Kochba, Judea had two short years of independence.

In 1960, Yigal Yadin, professor of archaeology at the Hebrew University in Jerusalem, launched an expedition to explore the caves in the mountains near the Dead Sea. A member of the expedition, exploring one of the narrow tunnels of a cave, discovered a basket filled with objects. Further inspection revealed a treasure trove of artifacts which included sandals, knives, mirrors, jugs, bowls, and the greatest treasure of all—papyrus rolls containing about 40 letters from Bar Kochba.

Bar Kochba had special coins struck to commemorate Judea's newly won independence. One side of the coins showed the Temple gate with a star above it, the other side was inscribed with Bar Kochba's name and the date (ca. 131–132 C.E.).

Rome Strikes Again

When Hadrian learned that Judea had declared its independence, he summoned Severus, his most able general, who was then engaged in a campaign in Britain. Severus appeared in Judea with a powerful army. But in the mountain passes and valleys, Jewish fighters swooped down upon his men. The Romans were repeatedly ambushed and beaten, and Severus suffered heavy losses.

Hadrian now came to Judea in person, bringing reinforcements to replace those who had been killed. Hadrian had decided to use Judea as an object lesson for the many other subjugated nations that made up the Roman Empire. In the end, Severus was victorious. Suffering huge losses, his army doggedly followed the Jewish fighters into the rugged terrain where their strongholds were located, destroying them one by one.

Bar Kochba's Defeat / 135 C.E.

Bar Kochba and his brave fighters made a final stand in the mountain fortress of Betar, southwest of Jerusalem. The Jewish soldiers fought desperately, inflicting heavy losses on the Romans, but Severus' army was much larger, and in the end Betar fell.

The land of Judea was laid waste. Fifty fortresses had been destroyed and a thousand villages lay in ruins. Jerusalem was completely destroyed, and the Jewish population of the land had been decimated. Hundreds of thousands of Jews had been killed, just as many were sold into slavery. Many towns and villages were almost deserted. Within a few years non-Jews began moving in. Areas that had once been entirely Jewish soon became mixed; some even had a non-Jewish majority.

In Jerusalem, as was their custom, the Romans cleared away the rubble and plowed up the ground. On the site they built the new city Hadrian had planned—a heathen city with temples for the worship of Roman gods. It was named Aelia Capitolina.

The Romans concluded that the people of Judea derived their strength from their religion. If Torah study was outlawed and the religious leaders were eliminated, they reasoned, the ordinary people would yield to Roman authority. Accordingly, soldiers hunted down the most important leaders. Rabbi Akiva was condemned to be skinned alive. With his last breath, the saintly hero proclaimed the words of the Shema, "Hear, O Israel, the Lord is our God, the Lord is one."

A silver coin issued by the revolutionary government of Bar Kochba. He and his followers set up a Jewish state in 132–135 B.C.E. which was soon crushed by the Romans.

Judah HaNasi / *2nd century C.E.*

A Spiritual Center in Galilee / ca. 140 C.E.

When the Roman persecution came to an end, a new academy was founded in the Galilean town of Usha by Rabbi Judah ben Ilai, one of Akiva's students. It was patterned on the academy at Yavneh. The scholars who studied and taught at Usha were the heirs of the rabbis who had expounded the Torah at Yavneh. As had been the case after the first revolt, the nasi acted as spiritual head of the Jewish community and was recognized as patriarch by the Roman government.

Judah HaNasi

The literal meaning of the Hebrew word *nasi* is "prince." It was a very fitting title for the head of the Sanhedrin, for the nasi had to be a man of learning and fine character whose everyday life would set an example for the people. The nasi most beloved and best-remembered for these qualities was Judah HaNasi, known in English as Judah the Patriarch or Judah the Prince, and often referred to in Hebrew simply as "Rabbi." Judah succeeded his father, Simon, who became nasi after the second revolt, and held the office for almost 50 years.

An outstanding scholar, Judah HaNasi is regarded as the last of the tannaim, for with him the great tannaitic era came to an end. Judah HaNasi set up the Sanhedrin and the academy in Beth-She'arim, and later in Sepphoris. He was very eager to unify the scattered Jewish communities throughout the world. As nasi, he had the sole authority to ordain rabbis and judges even for posts in faraway lands.

A Byzantine mosaic from the 6th century synagogue of Beth-She'an.

Bar'am, high up in the mountains of Upper Galilee, is the site of the best-preserved ancient synagogue in the country, dating to the end of the 2nd or beginning of the 3rd century C.E.

With the destruction of Jerusalem in 70 C.E., Jewish political and military life was crushed. Only towards the end of the 2nd and beginning of the 3rd century, however, were Jews allowed to engage in serious rebuilding programs. This was due largely to the attitude of Emperor Septimius Severus, more benevolent than his predecessors and more tolerant toward the Jews of Palestine.

The Hebrew Language Survives

In Judah HaNasi's time, most Jews, even in the land of Israel, spoke Aramaic, the language of their neighbors, the non-Jewish peoples of Palestine, Babylonia, and Persia. Judah was greatly concerned about the survival of Hebrew. He wanted it to be a living language, used everyday in Jewish homes. To set an example, he and his household spoke only Hebrew. It was said that Judah's servants spoke better Hebrew than many scholars. He also composed his great law code of the Mishnah, in Hebrew.

Judah's love of the Torah and of Hebrew went hand in hand with wide cultural interests. He knew many languages. He spoke and read Greek and Latin, and was learned in many subjects. He had many non-Jewish friends, including Marcus Aurelius (121–180 C.E.), a Roman emperor who was very interested in philosophy.

The academy at Sepphoris was a great success. Students from Babylonia and other faraway places came there to study with Judah and his colleagues. He used to say, "I have learned much from my teachers, more from my colleagues, but most of all from my students." He gave freely of his wealth to needy students and scholars, and to the poor of the land.

Tombs of the Just—Joseph in Shechem, Saul in Gilboa, Rabbi Akiva in Tiberias, etc.—in the eyes of a Jewish pilgrim. Manuscript dating from 1598.

material—laws and legal decisions, biblical commentary, legends and historical narratives—had been accumulating. Some of this had been organized by Rabbi Akiva, but none of it had been set down in writing. Judah HaNasi knew that this material might be lost and forgotten unless it was put in writing.

Recording the Oral Tradition

Judah HaNasi dedicated his whole life to the great task of compiling, editing, and preserving the Oral Tradition. Over the centuries, a huge quantity of unwritten

After the destruction of Jerusalem in 70 C.E., the center of the Jewish religious and national life shifted to the Galilee. Beth-She'arim, about 10 miles from Haifa, became an important Jewish city. Rabbi Judah HaNasi made it the seat of the Sanhedrin. He also compiled the Mishnah there, and in 220 C.E. was buried there in the family tomb.

In 1953, Israeli archaeologists discovered a giant necropolis, an underground city of the dead. The numerous vaulted catacombs are cut out of the soft limestone hills around which the city was built.

After the destruction of Jerusalem, Jews could not use the traditional cemetery on the Mount of Olives, so the necropolis became the central burial ground. The necropolis is a series of long, vaulted interconnected catacombs with thousands of marble and stone coffins, some of which weigh up to five tons. The entrance to the underground city is from stone courtyards dug out of the hills. One of the catacombs contains burial sites with inscriptions that mention the talmudic sages Gamliel and Hanina.

The Oral Tradition

The Mishnah / 1st–2nd century C.E.

The Oral Tradition had grown to such a huge size that very few could possibly remember all of it. In years past, scholars had felt that putting the Oral Tradition in writing would violate the spirit of Jewish law, but now they believed that this step had to be taken if the Torah was to survive. With the assistance of his colleagues and students, Judah set to work on the great task. The entire Oral Tradition was edited and logically arranged according to subject. Around 200 C.E. it was finally put into a permanent written form that would ensure its survival. The work that resulted from their efforts is called the Mishnah. Several centuries later the Mishnah became the basis of the vast encyclopedia of Jewish law and lore known as the Talmud.

In this gigantic task, Judah and his colleagues were aided by the contributions of earlier scholars. Since the time of Yohanan ben Zakkai and the academy at Yavneh, efforts had been made to organize some of the vast material of the Oral Tradition.

In the days of the tannaim, it had been customary in legal discussions to refer to the decisions of Hillel, or the decisions of Shammai, or the decisions of other scholars. Rabbi Akiva and Rabbi Meir were not content with this personalized way of classifying decisions, and proceeded to organize them instead on the basis of what area of law they referred to.

Divisions of the Mishnah

Judah HaNasi codified the legal commentaries and decisions of the Oral Tradition according to subject matter, grouping them into six main divisions:

1. Zeraim (Seeds): Laws of agriculture & prayer.
2. Mo'ed (Festivals): The observance of the Sabbath, festivals and fast days.
3. Nashim (Women): Marriage and divorce.
4. Nezikin (Damages): Civil and criminal laws.
5. Kodashim (Holy Matters): Temple services, sacrifices, and Shehitah (Kosher slaughter).
6. Tohorot (Purities): Ritual purity and cleanliness.

Each of these divisions in turn is subdivided into tractates (*masekhtot*), chapters (*perakim*), and paragraphs (*mishnayot*).

The End of an Era

For many years Judah HaNasi suffered from a painful ailment, but he worked on and devoted himself fully to this task. He also continued with his teaching and other activities. When Judah died around 220 C.E., he was mourned deeply by his friends, colleagues, and students, and indeed by the whole community of Israel. He was one of those rare men who embodied the spirit of a kind father for an entire people. "Not since Moses," the people said, "has there been a man like Judah, who so combines leadership with Torah." Crowds of people paid the last honors as Judah's body was brought to burial at Beth-She'arim. Everyone seemed to feel that a great era of Jewish history had come to an end.

With the death of Judah HaNasi the period of the tannaim ended. The work of the tannaim was preserved in the Mishnah, which served as a groundwork of Jewish law for generations to come.

Rabbi Heller

Rabbi Bertinoro

This page from a manuscript of the Mishnah was written between the 12th and 14th centuries.

A page from tractate Ketubot. The Mishnah is in the center. To the right is the commentary of Rabbi Obadiah Bertinoro, who lived in Italy and then in Jerusalem in the 15th century. To the left is the commentary of Rabbi Yomtov Lipman Heller, of the 17th century.

Halakhah: A Way of Life

The rabbis from the time of Yohanan ben Zakkai to that of Judah HaNasi are known as tannaim, which means "teachers" in Aramaic. The period in which they lived and worked is called the tannaitic age. During this period, with all hope of Jewish independence destroyed as a result of the two disastrous revolts, the center of Jewish life changed from governmental institutions to religious institutions like the synagogue and the academy. The nation's religious leaders formulated a body of regulations for daily life. These regulations are called halakhot.

The word halakhot is the plural of halakhah, which comes from the Hebrew verb *halakh*, meaning "to walk." The halakhot are a series of laws that teach observant Jews how to "walk" through life. By observing the halakhot, all of which ultimately derive from the Torah, the pious Jew lives in accordance with God's will.

The scholars in Israel and Babylonia who followed the tannaim are known as amoraim, which means "spokesmen" or "interpreters." The period in which they were active extended from the 3rd through the 6th century C.E.

Yohanan and Simeon

Yohanan bar Nappaha / 225 C.E.

One of the outstanding scholars in the academy at Tiberias was Yohanan bar Nappaha. The son of a blacksmith, Yohanan was a disciple of Judah HaNasi. He helped to establish a satisfactory method for studying the Mishnah and commenting on its sources. He was much admired by Jewish scholars everywhere.

Simeon ben Lakish / 225 C.E.

One day, Yohanan bar Nappaha met a stranger who impressed him very much. The stranger was a man of outstanding physical appearance, strongly athletic and full of vitality. His name was Simeon ben Lakish. Simeon told Yohanan that he had once been thrown into the arena with Roman gladiators, and had survived. He also had been a trainer of wild animals. Simeon talked at length about his many experiences. He even hinted that he had been the head of a band of highwaymen.

Eventually, Yohanan persuaded Simeon to change his way of life and join him in the academy. Simeon ben Lakish followed this new road and in time became a great rabbi. Many of his discussions with Yohanan on important points of Torah interpretation were recorded by later scholars. There is a romantic side to the story. Simeon married Yohanan's beautiful sister.

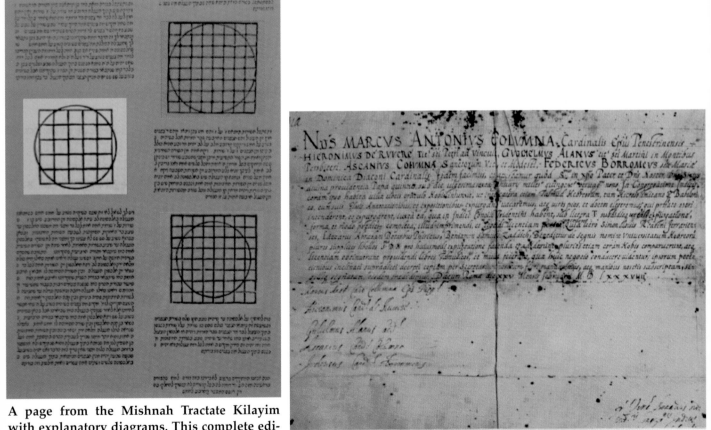

A page from the Mishnah Tractate Kilayim with explanatory diagrams. This complete edition of the Mishnah was printed by Soncino in Naples, Italy in 1492

Pope Sixtus V, in 1589 ordered the censorship of the Mishnah, the Talmud, and other Jewish books. Above is the Pope's edict.

Roman Christianity

Constantine Embraces Christianity / 285–337 C.E.

Developments in Israel were interrupted by an event which deeply affected Jews everywhere: the Roman emperor, Constantine, embraced Christianity. By the year 300 C.E. there were so many Christians in the Roman Empire that the emperor found it politically advantageous to seek Christian support.

With the power of the government behind them, the Christians set out to

The Arch of Constantine in Rome. This arch is decorated with panels and statues taken from other monuments from the reigns of Trajan and Hadrian.

Byzantine coin with a likeness of Emperor Constantine the Great. Constantine converted to Christianity and established his capital at Byzantium, which he rebuilt as a purely Christian city, renamed Constantinople.

destroy Judaism. They regarded it as a rival religion and resented the fact that the Jews, among whom Jesus had first lived and preached, had never accepted the new faith built around him.

Constantine was soon persuaded to enforce a series of anti-Jewish laws. The empire had become weak, and he thought that its strength might be revived if its people were united under the Christian banner. Looking with disfavor on Judaism, he sought to undermine it.

Under Constantine II, Constantine's son, new anti-Jewish laws were issued and a revolt broke out among the Jews of Galilee. The Romans crushed the uprising, destroying Sepphoris and Tiberias, the seats of the academies. Everywhere, Jews had to flee for their lives.

A Period of Peace

In 361 C.E., Constantine's successor, Julian the Apostate, treated the Jews more kindly. The academies were reopened and peace again reigned in the land. Julian had rejected Christianity and hoped to restore paganism to its former dominance. He did everything he could to weaken Christianity. He even sent a letter to the nasi, Hillel II, in which he addressed him as his "Venerable Brother, the Patriarch," and announced that he intended to rebuild the Holy Temple.

Christianity the Official Religion

Julian's reign was short, and after his death in 363 C.E. the Roman Empire again came under the rule of a Christian emperor. Henceforth, Christianity was the empire's official religion. Many other restrictive laws forced the Jews into a position of disadvantage. They were forbidden to own Christian slaves. Intermarriage between Jews and Christians was also forbidden.

In 399 C.E. the government prohibited the sending of emissaries (*apostoli*) to Jewish communities in other parts of the empire to raise funds to support institutions in Palestine.

The Gemara

The Talmud

In the days of Hillel II's son, Gamaliel V, and grandson, Judah IV, the end of Jewish authority in Palestine drew near. Working under great pressure, the last of the Palestinian amoraim collected and codified all the important legal discussions, teachings, and decisions that had taken place in Palestine since the completion of the Mishnah. This work was called the Gemara. The Mishnah and Gemara together make up the Talmud; the Mishnah is the foundation; the Gemara, the superstructure.

The Amoraim

Outside of Palestine, new academies were rising and flourishing in the faraway land of Babylonia. In the town of Nehardea, two students of Judah HaNasi, Rav and Samuel, started to teach and make independent decisions. They based their work on the Mishnah. The generations of scholars after Judah HaNasi, both in Palestine and in Babylonia, were called amoraim, meaning "speakers" or "interpreters." A wealth of new discussions, decisions, stories, and allegories accumulated, both in Galilee and in the new academies of Babylonia. Many Babylonian scholars still went to the academy at Tiberias in Palestine to study with the masters and judges of the academy and the Sanhedrin.

The Palestinian and Babylonian Talmuds

There are two versions of the Talmud, one compiled in Palestine, the other in Babylonia. Both of them are built upon the Mishnah, but the Palestinian Gemara, the work of the Palestinian amoraim, is shorter and does not cover all the tractates of the Mishnah. The Babylonian Gemara, the work of the amoraim in Babylonia, is much more extensive. The Palestinian Talmud (sometimes called the Jerusalem Talmud) was completed around 400 C.E. The Babylonian Gemara continued to grow for another century.

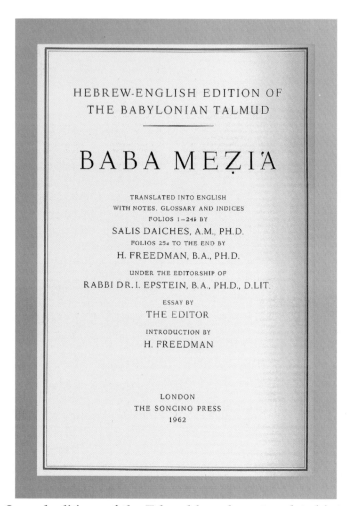

HEBREW-ENGLISH EDITION OF
THE BABYLONIAN TALMUD

BABA MEZIA

TRANSLATED INTO ENGLISH
WITH NOTES, GLOSSARY AND INDICES
FOLIOS 1–24b BY
SALIS DAICHES, A.M., PH.D.
FOLIOS 25a TO THE END BY
H. FREEDMAN, B.A., PH.D.

UNDER THE EDITORSHIP OF
RABBI DR. I. EPSTEIN, B.A., PH.D., D.LIT.

ESSAY BY
THE EDITOR

INTRODUCTION BY
H. FREEDMAN

LONDON
THE SONCINO PRESS
1962

Several editions of the Talmud have been translated into English. This is one of the title pages of the Soncino edition, published in England.

In 1923 Rabbi Meir Shapiro decided to found a course of Talmud study which he called Daf Yomi. The word *daf* means "page" and *yomi* means "daily." Rabbi Shapiro's plan envisaged the study of all 2711 pages (*dapim*) of the Talmud in seven and a quarter years.

Today, many people all over the world participate in the Daf Yomi program. Some study the Talmud individually, some in groups which use both the original and the English translation. There are Daf Yomi groups in Hollywood, the Senate in Washington, and the boardrooms of Wall Street.

The heading starts with the page number, the name of the chapter, the number of the chapter, and the name of the tractate.

אלו מציאות פרק שני בבא מציעא

Rashi, whose full name was Rabbi Solomon ben Isaac, was an eleventh century French scholar. Rashi's commentary on the Talmud is one of the most influential contributions to rabbinic literature ever written.

The text of the Talmud consists of the Mishnah and the Gemara. The Mishnah is the six-part legal code which was developed in Israel during the first and second centuries C.E. It was written in Hebrew and was completed by Rabbi Yehudah Ha-Nasi. The Gemara is written in Aramaic and is a summary of the legal debates on the meaning of the Mishnah. It was compiled in the Babylonian academies between the third and sixth centuries C.E.

This commentary to the Talmud, called *Ayn Mishpat*, lists the sources of the laws and quotations cited in the Talmud. *Ner Mitzvah* lists the legal literature relevant to the talmudic passage.

The disciples of Rashi, called Tosafists, lived in the twelfth, thirteenth, and fourteenth centuries, and composed a talmudic commentary called Tosafot. The word "Tosafot" means commentary.

This is a commentary on the Talmud by Rabbenu (Hananel ben Hushi'el). Rabbenu lived in Kairouan, Morocco, in the tenth and eleventh centuries.

There are numerous other commentaries in this edition of the Talmud, but they do not appear on this page.

A page of the Talmud with some of the commentaries. The selection is from Baba Batra, first tractate of the Order Nezikin.

The Byzantine Empire

The Split in the Roman Empire / 303 C.E.

Although the Roman Empire had one official religion, Christianity, it was torn by strife and disunited. In the 4th century C.E. the empire was divided in two for administrative purposes. The western part had its capital at Rome. The eastern part had its capital in the city of Byzantium, which was rebuilt and renamed Constantinople. The eastern portion of the Roman Empire soon became an independent entity, the Byzantine Empire.

The End of the Patriarchate

The governing apparatus of the Jewish community of Palestine was headed by the nasi, who had been given the title of patriarch by the Romans. It was supported by contributions from Jewish communities throughout the Roman Empire. After the empire was divided, however, the western Roman government prohibited fund-raising by Palestinian emissaries in order to prevent money from being drained off to an area under Byzantine control.

Deprived of financial support, the nasi, the academy, and the Sanhedrin became impoverished. When Gamaliel VI died in 426 C.E., leaving no sons, the Byzantine emperor, Theodosius II, decided to abolish the patriarchate. This was the end of Jewish autonomy in Palestine, and under

During the Byzantine period, numerous churches were built in Israel. Above is a photo of the ruins of the 6th century church of St. Theodorus at Avdat.

Byzantine rule it now became a Christian country. Some of its remaining Jewish inhabitants emigrated to Babylon or other places, but many continued to live there even under the increasingly adverse conditions.

Although there were still Jews living in Palestine, the spiritual leadership of world Jewry now passed to the Babylonian Jewish community. Babylonia was a rich, fertile country situated between the Tigris and Euphrates rivers. Jews had been living there ever since 597 B.C.E., when Nebuchadnezzar had deported thousands of people after he conquered Jerusalem.

The Byzantines discovered the secret of making flamethrowers. By 675 C.E. the Byzantine fleets with their deadly flamethrowers had won control of the seas. In the 9th century the Arabs also learned the secret and used flamethrowers against the Christian crusaders.

Babylonian Jewry

The Babylonian Jewish community had grown and prospered. By the 1st century C.E. there were more Jews in Babylon than in Judea. The Babylonian Jews maintained their own synagogues, their own houses of study, and their own courts where Jewish law was observed.

Palestine as Spiritual Center

Like Jews everywhere, the Jews of Babylonia regarded Palestine as the spiritual center of Judaism. Babylonian students, including the great Hillel, flocked to the teachers in Jerusalem. After the destruction of the Second Temple, Jews from Babylonia continued to study with the tannaim at Yavneh, Tiberias, and Sepphoris.

In Roman times Babylonia was ruled by the Parthians, able warriors from Persia who had conquered the old Seleucid kingdom. They were tolerant toward the Jews, and welcomed the stream of refugees from Judea who poured in after each of the revolts against Rome.

The Exilarch

The Jewish community in Babylonia was headed by an official known as the *resh galuta*, meaning "leader of the exile." The office of the exilarch, as it is often called, was hereditary, and the exilarchs were descendants of King David, tracing their descent back through Jehoiachin, who was king of Judea at the time of Nebuchadnezzar.

The exilarch ruled over all the Jewish communities in Babylonia, collecting the taxes assessed by the government as well as the taxes the Jews imposed on themselves to support their communal institutions. Until its destruction in 70 C.E., the exilarch also collected the voluntary tax Jews everywhere paid to support the Temple. In addition, the exilarch had the authority to supervise markets and schools, maintain law and order in predominantly Jewish towns, and enforce rulings by Jewish courts. The exilarch was, in short, the powerful ruler of a rich and important autonomous community.

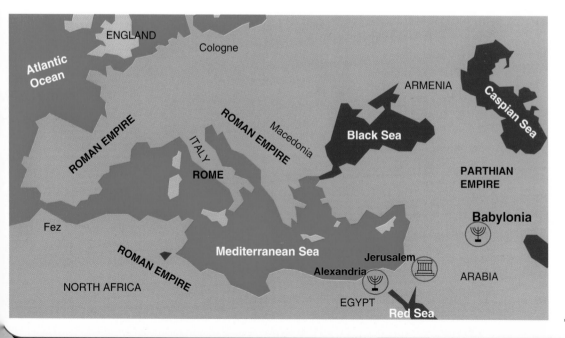

The largest Jewish communities are circled Alexandria in Egypt; the land of Israel; and Babylonia.

Rav and Samuel

Abba Arikha / early 3rd cent. C.E.

In the early centuries, Babylonian Jewry's brightest young men went to study in Palestine, and as a result there were not enough trained rabbis and scholars to staff the schools and religious institutions it needed. One of these young Babylonians, Abba Arikha (Abba the Tall), was among the most gifted of Judah HaNasi's students. Abba Arikha is usually known simply as Rav, meaning "Master." (Rav eventually became the title of all ordained rabbis.)

When Rav returned to Babylonia, he brought with him a copy of the newly composed Mishnah. Rav was appointed inspector of markets and of weights and measures for the Jewish communities of Babylonia. As he journeyed through the land, he saw how slack the people's spiritual life had become. He began to reorganize the schools and synagogues. Eventually, he was appointed head of the academy at Nehardea, but he declined this post so that it could be given to a younger colleague, Mar Samuel, also known as Samuel Yarhina'ah (Samuel the Astronomer), another gifted student of Judah HaNasi.

Rav went on to found an academy of his own in Sura, near the city of Pumpeditha. His new school attracted many scholars and students.

The Month of Kallah

Rav instituted a revolutionary new plan of study, open to anyone who wanted to take advantage of it. Every year during the months of Adar (March-April) and Elul (September), when the farmers could be spared from their work and when artisans and merchants could take a rest during their slack season, Rav would give a special course in Jewish law. These months were called the months of Kallah ("Assembly").

During the months of Kallah and the weeks preceding the holidays, people would stream into Sura from all corners of the surrounding provinces to attend the popular courses at the academy. A thirst for learning took hold of Babylonian Jewry; throughout the land synagogues and schoolhouses were improved and Jews met in great numbers to study and learn.

With the help of the Mishnah, Babylonian scholars were able to apply the Torah's teachings to life in exile. By introducing the Mishnah to their students, Rav and Samuel succeeded in their great purpose of making the Torah a living guide that would enable the Jews of Babylonia to deal with the many problems they faced.

Fragment of an ancient manuscript Siddur showing the Ahabah Rabbah prayer.

The Siddur Is Revised

Samuel and Rav remained close friends and collaborators throughout their lives. Together, they revised the Siddur (prayerbook). Rav wrote the beautiful Alenu prayer for Rosh Hashanah; it is still part of our daily service. Samuel wrote a shorter version of the Shemoneh Esreh (or Amidah)—the Eighteen Benedictions.

Mar Samuel / ca. 177–257 C.E.

Samuel's last years were darkened by trouble. In 226 C.E., the Parthians were overthrown by the Persians. The new rulers of Babylonia were Zoroastrians. Their priests tried to force their religion on all the inhabitants of the territories they had conquered. Since the Jews were not willing to accept Zoroastrianism, a time of persecution began.

After Samuel's death, Nehardea was plundered by desert invaders. Nehardea never regained its former importance. Its academy was rebuilt, but the centers of Jewish learning were thenceforth at Sura and Pumpeditha.

The fire altar depicted on this Sasanian coin was the focal point of Zoroastrian religion. These perpetually burning fires were set up all over Iran. Some burned in the open air, while others were enclosed in fire-temples.

A relief from Persepolis dating from the early Second Temple period depicts Ahura Mazda, god of Zoroastrianism, the religion of ancient Persia. Zoroastrianism taught that the world was torn between two deities: Ahura Mazda, the Wise Lord, creator of heaven and earth, light and life, who embodied the spirit of goodness, truth, and law; and Ahriman, the Evil Spirit, whose essence was falsehood and death.

Rava and Abaye / *early 4th century*

The Academy of Pumpeditha attracted the brightest and most dedicated students in Palestine and Babylon. The methodology and sharp disputations between the amoraim (teachers) and the students created keen, knowledgeable scholars who made great contributions to halakhic principles.

Among the students were two colleagues, Rava and Abaye, who became the two greatest amoraim of the 4th century.

Abaye / 4th century

Abaye, orphaned as a child, was raised by his uncle, Rabbi bar Nahmani, who lovingly nicknamed him Abaye, meaning "Little Father." Abaye perpetuated the memory of his foster-mother, whom he referred to as "Em," by publicly quoting her proverbs and folk remedies.

In the field of halakhah and Torah learning, Abaye emphasized the importance of traditional sources. He supported the plain meaning of the biblical text (*peshat*) against the midrashic (non-literal) interpretation.

Abaye was known for his willingness to help others. He took special pride when one of his students satisfactorily completed a section of the Mishnah. Although he was poor, he would make a party to celebrate the event, so as to encourage the student. His peaceloving disposition is recalled by the saying "Be mild in speech, suppress your anger, and maintain goodwill to everyone."

Abaye headed the Academy in Pumpeditha from 333 to 338 C.E., at which point he was succeeded by his boyhood friend Rava.

Rava / 4th century

Rava, the son of Rabbi Joseph bar Ham, married a granddaughter of the great talmudic sage Rav, who founded the academy in Sura. His real name was Abba, but he was called Rava, which is the contraction of Rabbi plus Abba. In addition to being a brilliant scholar, Rava worked hard to maintain good relations with the Persian government.

Rava was on friendly terms with the exilarch of Persia, King Shapur II's intermediary in dealing with the Jewish community. He also enjoyed the special protection of Shapur because he had secretly contributed large sums of money to the king. As a result, Rava succeeded in easing the oppression against the Jews of Babylonia.

The debates between the two Talmud luminaries which formed the foundation of halakhah are known as "the investigation of Rava and Abaye." Eventually these debates became a major part of the Babylonian Talmud.

This drinking bowl dates from the 7th century. It depicts King Shapur II on a hunt.

Later scholars, who studied the debates, decided all the cases in favor of Rava except for six which were won by Abaye. It is thought that Rava's conclusions and thought patterns were more logical and clearer than Abaye's.

Abaye (333–338 C.E.) and Rava (338–352) successively headed the academy at Pumpeditha. Both amoraim, because of their brilliance, drew the brightest minds of Palestine and Babylonia to their academies.

THE TALMUDIC AGE

SOFERIM (scribes) **5th to 3rd cent. B.C.E.**	The generations of scholars and teachers who carried on the work of EZRA.
ZUGOT (pairs) **2nd cent. B.C.E. to** **about 10 C.E.**	The two leaders of the great Sanhedrin who carried on the teachings and interpretations of the Torah after the period of the Soferim. HILLEL and SHAMMAI were the last and most brilliant of the Zugot.

TANNAIM (Teachers)
 1st and 2nd cent. C.E.
	The scholars and teachers whose works are recorded in the Mishnah.
	     GAMALIEL I, Nasi and last president of the Great Sanhedrin.
	     YOHANAN BEN ZAKKAI, founder of the academy of Yavneh.
	     GAMALIEL II, Nasi and head of the Sanhedrin and of the
	         academy of Yavneh.
	     RABBI AKIBA.
	     RABBI MEIR and SIMEON BAR YOHAI.
	     JUDAH HANASI (Judah I), Nasi, head of the Sanhedrin and
	         the academy, compiler of the Mishnah.

AMORAIM (speakers)
 3rd to 6th cent. C.E.
 (about 200-499)
	The scholars and teachers whose work is recorded in the Gemara.
	     GAMALIEL III, son of Judah Hanasi, head of the academy
	         and of the Sanhedrin.
	     ABBA ARIKHA (RAV) and MAR SAMUEL founded the
	         Babylonian Talmud.
	     YOHANAN BAR NAPPAHA and SIMEON BEN LAKHISH.
	     HILLEL II, Nasi and head of the academy and of the Sanhedrin,
	         introduced the fixed calendar.
	     Completion of the Palestinian Talmud.
	     GAMALIEL IV, last Nasi. End of Patriarchate.
	     ASHI and
	     RABINA, compiled the Babylonian Talmud.

SABORAIM (reasoners) **500 to 530 C.E.**	The scholars and teachers who completed the editing of the Babylonaian Talmud. Until the tiime of the Gaonate great Babylonian scholars bore the title of SABORA.

Rav Ashi / *ca. 352–427 C.E.*

The troubled Jewish community of Babylonia found a new leader in Rav Ashi, a highly gifted scholar of a noble and wealthy family. When still a young man, he had been appointed head of the academy of Sura. He immediately set about revising the course of study and making it more meaningful to his listeners. Again people streamed into Sura during the Kallah months and before the holidays.

The Babylonian Talmud

Rav Ashi also turned his attention to the Gemara that had been developed by the amoraim of Babylonia. Aided by his students and colleagues, he codified this vast accumulation of oral material according to the system used in the Mishnah by Judah HaNasi. During the months of Kallah, many students contributed their own discussions and decisions, together with stories and allegories they had heard from earlier teachers.

For 60 years Rav Ashi presided over the academy of Sura, earning the distinction of being called Rabbana, "Our Master," an honorary title ordinarily conferred only on the exilarchs.

Rabina succeeds Rav Ashi / 427 C.E.

After Rav Ashi's death a time of persecution began again under a cruel Persian king. Rabina, who succeeded Ashi as head of the academy of Sura, con-tinued the work of editing and codifying, but it took another generation of scholars to complete the work. This next generation, known as the saboraim ("reasoners") further edited the Babylonian Gemara. By the year 530 C.E. the Babylonian Talmud, consisting of the Babylonian Gemara together with the Mishnah, was completed.

The Gaonim

In 531 C.E. a new king, Khosru I, ascended the throne of Persia. During his reign the academies of Sura and Pumpeditha reopened. From then on, the heads of the great academies were called gaonim, the plural form of *gaon* ("excellency"). Since the patriarchate in the land of Israel had come to an end, the gaonim were the spiritual leaders of world Jewry. In the reopened academies the newly completed Babylonian Talmud was studied and became the basis for further work.

A productive new period of Jewish life began. The Persian Empire was at peace. Its people prospered, and its cities were filled with beautiful gardens and palaces. Poets and painters, architects and sculptors, created many beautiful works. Craftsmen fashioned handsome objects of metalwork and made lovely materials of cloth and silk. After the death of Khosru II in 628 C.E., however, Persia went into a decline.

Magic bowl with Hebrew inscription found in the ruins of Babylon.

The Jews of Arabia

Jews had settled in Arabia as early as 70 C.E., when the Second Temple was destroyed. Escaping from the devastation brought on by the first revolt against Rome, some of them settled on the oases in the northwestern part of the Arabian peninsula, where they became farmers and planters. According to some sources, it was orchard keepers and planters from Judea who first introduced the date palm to Arabia. Jewish settlers also helped found the cities which lay along the strip of oases through which merchant caravans laden with precious incense and spices traveled between east and west. Jewish merchants and artisans sold their wares in the cities of Yathrib and Mecca.

A Passover Seder as conducted by a Yemenite family.

The Kingdom of Yemen

In Yemen, in the southwestern corner of Arabia, Jewish planters and artisans helped to bring wealth and prosperity to the land. Many Jews settled there, and in the 5th century C.E., the king became a convert to Judaism. The Jewish kingdom of Yemen flourished. Its merchants traded goods in many lands, its artisans forged lovely vessels of silver, copper, and gold, and its poets wrote beautiful songs. In 525 C.E., however, the Jewish kingdom was destroyed by the Byzantines and the Abyssinians. Although many Jews left Yemen, a sizable Jewish community remained there.

In 575, Yemen became part of the Persian Empire, but the Jewish community never regained its former splendor. Often there was bitter poverty and persecution. In spite of these hardships, the Yemenite Jews held fast to their beliefs and preserved their skills. They continued to do fine metalwork, and to plant and trade.

A page from an illuminated Yemenite Five Books of Moses. This manuscript was completed in 1496 C.E for Ibrahim ibn Yusuf ibn Sa'id ibn Ibrahim al-Israili. The text is a section of the Song of Moses.

Islam Begins / 570 C.E.

Meanwhile, in the deserts of Arabia, a new power was preparing for conquest---a people driven on by a new religion and a need for fertile land.

The Rise of Muhammad / ca. 570–632 C.E.

Around the end of the 6th century, an Arab camel driver named Muhammad was profoundly influenced by the concepts of Judaism. Although Muhammad was poor and uneducated, he possessed extraordinary intelligence and energy. He worked his way up untiringly until he became a caravan master, and eventually one of the wealthy merchants and importers of the city of Mecca.

Like other Arabs, Muhammad believed himself to be a descendant of Abraham, the patriarch of the Jews, through Ishmael, his elder son. Deeply occupied with religious questions, Muhammad began to develop his own ideas. Finally he came to look upon himself as a great prophet like Moses and the prophets of old. Muhammad

An old painting showing Muhammad preaching to the non-believers.

affirmed the belief in the one God, whom he called Allah. "There is no god but Allah, and Muhammad is his prophet," he declared. He proclaimed a new religion, and devoted all his intelligence and energy to the task of spreading it. Muhammad called his new religion Islam, meaning "submission" to the will of God.

A New Religion

The religion of Islam was founded on the basic principles of Judaism. Muhammad's prophecies contain pronouncements against idol worship and sacrifice, and uphold the worship of one God. He promised his followers that if they followed the commandments of Islam they would be rewarded with eternal bliss in an afterlife in heaven.

Muhammad won no following in his own city of Mecca. The people there were enraged at his attempt to convert them to Islam and considered him a fanatical rabble-rouser. In the year 622 C.E. Muhammad was forced to flee from his home.

The Hegira (flight) of Muhammad was the key event in Muslim history. It was so important that on the Muslim calendar, all dates are A.H. ("year of the Hegira"). Thus, 1 A.H. is the same as 622 C.E.

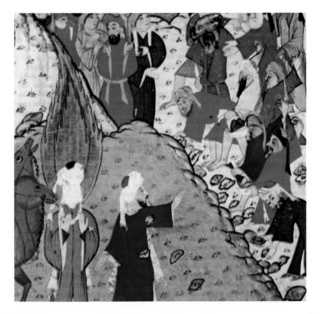

This 16th century Turkish painting shows an angry mob of the citizens of Mecca throwing stones at Muhammad. Because of their opposition he was forced to flee the city, but eight years later he returned in triumph. Note the halo around Muhammad's featureless face.

127

The golden dome of the Mosque of Omar in Jerusalem is a highly visible landmark. It was built by Caliph Abdul Malik Ibn Marwan in 691 C.E.

Islam Spreads

Muhammad preached his faith and sought followers among the many Arab tribes. Gradually the new religion took root throughout the Arabian peninsula. Yathrib, to which Muhammad fled when he was driven out of Mecca, became a holy city and was renamed Medina (Medinat-en-Navi, "City of the Prophet"). Mecca, his birthplace and long regarded as holy even before the advent of Islam, became the main shrine and object of pilgrimage for his followers.

Limits for the Jews of Arabia

Muhammad expected the Jews of Arabia to accept his new religion. After all, had it not been founded on the principles of Judaism, and was not he, Muhammad, a prophet in the great tradition of the prophets of Israel? When the Arabs of Mecca rejected Muhammad and he fled to Medina, he expected to find a friendly reception among the three Jewish tribes in the area. But the Jews of Medina rejected him.

Muhammad angrily abandoned the effort to convert the Jews and changed the direction of Muslim prayer from Jerusalem to Mecca. When he attained power he revenged himself on the Jewish tribes. Some were put to death, some were sold as slaves, and some were forced to convert. Those who survived, together with the Jews of Yemen, were taxed excessively and forced to obey humiliating laws.

The 29 letters of the Arabic alphabet. Each letter is accompanied by its Arabic name and sound. Arabic, like Hebrew, is written from right to left.

Jews (wearing their traditional colored costumes) consult a 120-year-old elder in Damascus, who tells them that Muhammad was a Messiah and the last prophet to come into the world—a 16th century Turkish miniature based on 10th century Arab text. In this period there was constant theological discussion about the respective roles of the three monotheistic religions—Judaism, Christianity, and Islam.

The Holy Wars

Muhammad died in the year 632. His successors held the title of caliph. Muhammad was succeeded by Caliph Abu Bakr, who died two years later and was followed by Caliph Omar. As princely ruler of Arabia and religious leader of all Muslims, Omar declared a holy war. He and his followers rode across the desert into the lands of the Fertile Crescent. His army, recruited from all over Arabia, was made up of warriors united and fanatical in their faith.

Jerusalem Conquered / 638 C.E.
Omar and his generals conquered Egypt, Palestine, Syria, and Persia, spreading the faith of Islam in those lands. Omar laid the foundation of a vast Arab empire, often referred to as the caliphate. The Muslim empire ultimately spread over the entire

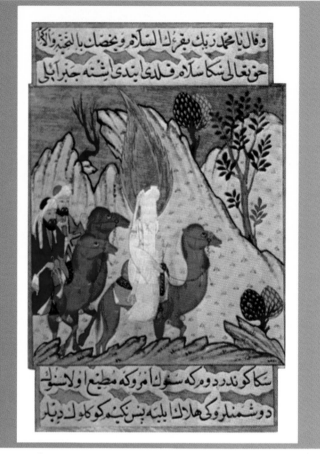

A page from an ancient copy of the Koran. Illuminated copies of the Koran were skillfully handwritten and illustrated in gold and bright colors.

An ancient painting showing Muhammad with the leader of a Jewish tribe in Arabia. He condemned the whole tribe to death because they refused to convert to the Muslim religion.

Fertile Crescent, across North Africa to Spain, and from the Nile delta eastward as far as India.

The Koran
During the reign of Omar's successor, Caliph Othman (644–656 C.E.), a son-in-law of Muhammad, the Koran, Islam's holy book, was put together in written form.

At Othman's command, all of Muhammad's prophecies were arranged and written down, based on notes taken by Muhammad's secretary at his master's dictation. The Koran is divided into chapters arranged in order of length. Written in beautiful classical Arabic, it begins with a short passage in praise of Allah.

The Nonbelievers

As the new Arab Empire grew, a body of laws known as the Pact of Omar was instituted in 640 C.E. to regulate Muslim relations with Jews and Christians. The rights of "nonbelievers" were severely reduced. They were forced to pay a humiliating poll tax; they were not allowed to ride on horseback and were forced to wear clothes that would make them conspicuous and set them apart from Muslims; and they were not permitted to bear arms. But they were not forbidden to observe their own religion.

As time passed, the Arab conquerors became more tolerant. The Jews of the Arab Empire followed their religion and way of life. Jewish poets wrote Arabic poetry, and Jewish physicians, mathematicians, and astronomers contributed to the growth of the sciences. Jewish merchants helped establish trade routes throughout the Middle East. They followed the Arab conquerors into North Africa, and eventually across the Mediterranean to far-off Spain.

A pilgrim caravan on the way to Mecca. The happy pilgrims are accompanied by music of horns and drums. Painted in 1237, in Baghdad.

Palestine Under the Caliphate

After Omar's conquest of Palestine in 638 C.E., conditions there improved. The Arabs established a Muslim sanctuary in Jerusalem, which had now become holy to three religions. Once again the Jews were permitted to enter the city and pray at the ruined western wall of the Temple. Soon there was a small Jewish community in Jerusalem.

The holy city of Mecca and its mosque. Near the center of the mosque is a small shrine called the Kaaba. Muslims believe that the Kaaba was built by Abraham and Ishmael. In the Kaaba is a black stone. Muslims believe the stone was given to Adam by an angel. Each year thousands of Muslim pilgrims come from far away to kiss the sacred black stone.

Timeline—The Age of Learning

JEWISH HIGHLIGHTS

Great Assembly of --- 250 BCE	**Rededication of Temple** 164 BCE	**Judea expels Syrians** 134 BCE	**Jerusalem Falls** 63BCE	**Herod the Great** 37 BCE	**Birth of Christianity** first century CE	**Jerusalem Falls** 70 CE

JEWISH • EVENTS PERSONALITIES • LITERATURE • HOLIDAYS

Septuaguint	Maccabean revolt	High priest, SIMON	Civil war	Temple enlarged	John the Baptist	Zealots
Bible standardized	JUDAH MACCABE	Sadducees	Judea becomes Roman province	Masada	Jesus crusified, 29 CE	Tish B'av
	Hanukah	Pharisees		Sanhedrin	Essenes	Johanan ben Zakkai
		Sanhedrin		Hillel	Dead Sea scrolls	
		Great Assembly		Shammai		
		Salome		Economic prosperity		

WORLD HISTORY

Alexander the Great	Selucid empire	Syria	Romans	Romans	Romans	Romans
Ptolemies	Antiochus IV	Hellenism	Pompei	Parthians	Pontius Pilate	Vespasian
Antiochus III			Julius Caesar			Titus

Timeline—The Age of Learning

JEWISH HIGHLIGHTS

Masada falls 73 CE	**Sanhedrin** Nasi 85 C.E.	**Bar Kochba Revolt** 132 C.E.	**Tannaim** 1st–2nd century C.E.	**Amoraim** 3rd–6th century C.E.	**Age of Gaonim** starts 589 C.E.	**Arabs conquer Jerusalem** 638 C.E.

JEWISH EVENTS • PERSONALITIES • LITERATURE • HOLIDAYS

▶ Eleazar ben Yair	▶ Gamaliel II	▶ Bar Kochba	▶ Mishnah	▶ Yohanan bar Nappaha	▶ Babylonian Talmud	▶ Muhammad
▶ Jews commit suicide	▶ Prayer services	▶ Rabbi Akiva executed	▶ Responsa	▶ Simeon ben Lakish	▶ Exilarch	▶ Islam begins, 622
▶ Josephus	▶ Torah readings	▶ Betar falls, 135 C.E.	▶ Halakhah	▶ Rav	▶ Responsa	▶ Forced conversion of Jews
			▶ Judah HaNasi	▶ Samuel and Rav Ashi	▶ Halakhah	▶ Omar
			▶ Siddur	▶ End of Patriarchate	▶ Masorah	▶ Koran
				▶ Jerusalem Talmud		▶ Pact of Omar
				▶ Early synagogues		

WORLD HISTORY

▶ Romans	▶ Romans	▶ Romans	▶ Parthians and Persians	▶ Babylon	▶ Persia	▶ Muslims
▶ Trajan		▶ Severus	▶ Romans	▶ Byzantines		▶ Persia
▶ Hadrian				▶ Constantine		▶ Caliphate
				▶ Rome		

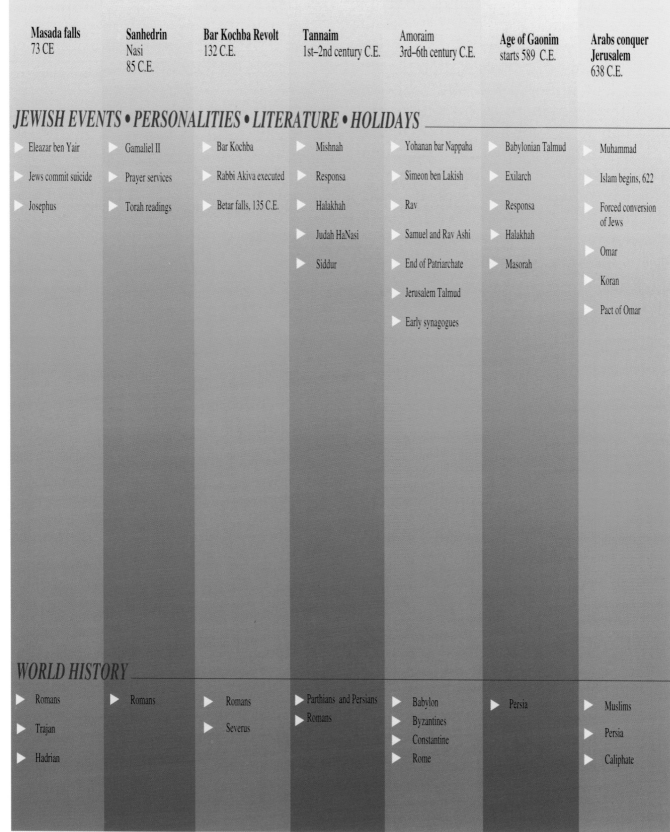

The Gaonim

Although the Jewish community in Jerusalem had been restored after the Muslim conquest, the center of Jewish life was still in Babylonia. Conditions had deteriorated during the persecution by the Persians, but under the Arabs, who conquered the area in 660, the situation of Babylonian Jewry improved. The schools of Sura and Pumpeditha reopened, presided over by the gaonim. Once again the Jewish community was led by the exilarch, a descendant of King David. The exilarchs were now authorized to collect taxes both for the caliphate and for the Jewish community. The gaonim was given the right to select the exilarch, but their choice had to be approved by the caliph.

Bustanai / ca. 620–675

The first exilarch under Muslim rule was Bustanai, a wise and beloved leader. The exilarchs who followed over many generations looked back to him as their spiritual ancestor. As heads of the academies, the gaonim had great prestige and often acted as advisors to the exilarchs, especially on matters of Jewish law and scholarship. Even the far-off communities of North Africa, Spain, and France turned to the gaonim for advice.

Whenever Jews anywhere were in doubt on questions of Jewish law (halakhah), they would send messengers to the gaonim in Babylonia. The Babylonian scholars sent their answers and legal decisions in clear, concise letters known as *teshuvot* (responsa). Ever since, decisions on legal questions by Jewish scholars have been set down in accordance with the form used in the gaonic responsa. Nowadays responsa are still written by prominent rabbis who are experts on the halakhah.

The Age of the Gaonim

The gaonic period extended from the 7th to the 11th century. During this era the gaonim sent emissaries to acquaint Jews in far-off communities with developments in Sura and Pumpeditha, and to teach the Talmud. By this means knowledge of the Talmud was spread far and wide, and a bond was established among the many groups that made up world Jewry.

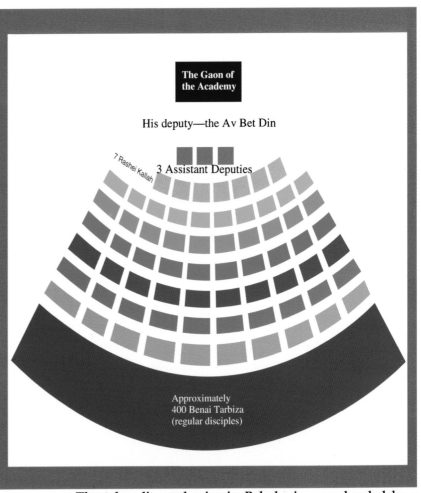

The talmudic academies in Babylonia were headed by a gaon. It consisted of 70 sages whose places in the hierarchy were fixed. The sages closer to the gaon, were generally the more advanced.

The Karaites / ca. 762 C.E.

In the 8th century a group opposed to the gaonim arose in Babylonia and became a powerful threat to Jewish unity. Its ideas resembled those of the Sadducees of old. This new movement rejected the Oral Tradition, claiming that the written Torah was the only valid source of Jewish law.

By rejecting the Oral Tradition, it was also rejecting the Talmud, in which the Oral Tradition had been codified.

Anan ben David / ca. 750

One of the foremost leaders of this movement was Anan ben David. As a member of the Davidic family, he had expected to become exilarch, but instead the gaonim of Pumpeditha and Sura chose his younger brother, Hananiah. Bitterly disappointed, Anan challenged his brother's right to the high office.

The caliph endorsed Hananiah as exilarch and, fearing unrest, had Anan arrested. Anan had to stand trial. On the advice of a Muslim lawyer, he testified that he did not care whether or not he became exilarch but was merely the founder of a new religion. As a result, he was acquitted.

Anan Combats the Talmud

Anan condemned the Talmud and the complicated legal system based upon it, emphasizing that every Jew had the right to interpret the Torah. For many people this approach had great appeal, even though its extreme form sometimes led to silly excesses. For example, the Talmud permitted the use of heat and light on the Sabbath if they were initiated before the Sabbath, but Anan did not. As a result, his followers were obliged to sit in the dark and cold on the day of rest.

Under Anan's successors, the movement he began named itself the Bnai Mikra ("Sons of the Scripture"). They were also called Karaites ("Scripturists").

In the 9th and 10th centuries the Karaite sect was an active, growing movement. Its leaders wrote eloquent defenses of their approach. Before long there were Karaites in Babylonia, Palestine, Egypt, and North Africa.

A 10th century Karaite manuscript of the Bible.

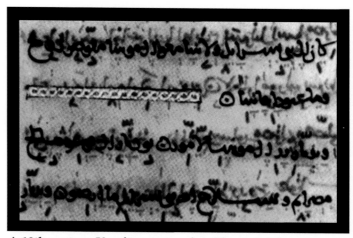

A 10th century Karaite manuscript. Through it is written in Hebrew and has vowel points, the characters are Arabic. Arab and Jewish cultures were closely linked in this period

Saadia Gaon / 882–942 C.E.

Saadia ben Joseph (882–942) was an Egyptian Jew. His brilliant treatises against Karaism helped many people to understand the issues at stake in the conflict between the new sect and talmudic tradition.

Saadia as Gaon

Concerned about the inroads being made by Karaism, the exilarch summoned Saadia to become the gaon of the academy at Sura. He proved to be the greatest, most capable of all the gaonim. During his tenure he taught a whole new generation of scholars and wrote numerous responsa dealing with religious and legal questions from Jews in many lands. In addition, he succeeded in exposing the weaknesses of Karaism and restoring faith in the talmudic tradition. As a result, the unity of world Jewry was preserved.

The Siddur

Saadia was an accomplished poet in both Arabic and Hebrew. He translated the Bible into Arabic and compiled one of the first Jewish prayerbooks. It was called the Siddur, meaning "order," as our prayerbooks are called today. Saadia's Siddur was a very important achievement, because until his time the synagogue service had no fixed order or content.

Saadia the Thinker

Saadia Gaon was a profound religious philosopher. One of his greatest works was *Sefer ha-Emunot ve-De'ot* ("The Book of Beliefs and Opinions"), it explains Judaism's fundamental beliefs and ideas. Written in Arabic, it was helpful to the many Jews in Arabic-speaking countries who no longer spoke or read Hebrew. In

To teach the alphabet to young Hebrew scholars, this book was produced in 10th century Egypt. This page was found in the Cairo Genizah.

the days of Saadia Gaon, the prestige and power of the gaonim reached their highpoint. After the death of the great master, however, the importance of the Babylonian schools slowly diminished, and with it the influence of the gaonim.

Title page of the *Emunot ve-De'ot* by Saadia Gaon. This edition was printed in 1562, in Constantinople.

The Masorah

An absorbing task that now occupied the scholars of Tiberias was the establishment of the Masorah. The term Masorah literally means "handing down." It designates the establishment of the correct, standard text of the Holy Scriptures, to be "handed down" to future generations. Establishing the correct text was necessary because in ancient times every copy of the Bible had to be written by hand, and over the centuries errors of various kinds had slipped in. The scholars who performed this task are called Masoretes. The Masoretic text is followed by soferim (scribes) to this day when they copy scrolls of the Torah.

Page from the *Rules of Accents* by Jacob ben Asher in the 10th century. This momentous work established the rules of punctuation and spelling in the Bible

True Text and True Meaning

In order to preserve the true text and meaning of the Scriptures, the Masoretes carefully compared different versions of each biblical book and decided which corresponded to the pure, original form. They laid down the text word for word, letter for letter, and worked out a system of punctuation. They devised a system of vowel signs to ensure that every word was pronounced properly. In addition, they provided a system of accentuation and punctuation that also serves as musical notation for the chanting of the Torah and other parts of the Bible in the synagogue.

The Masoretes were active from the 7th through the 10th century. Their most outstanding scholars were Ben Asher and Ben Naphtali.

Colophon of the Masoretic Codex of Moses ben Asher (897 C.E.).

The Golden Age / *10th–12th century*

Spain Is Conquered

The Moors of North Africa were converted to Islam when the wave of Arab conquest spread westward during the early years of the caliphate. Under their rule, the Jews of North Africa prospered. In the city of Kairouan, near the site of ancient Carthage, a talmudic academy was established and a center of learning flourished.

Spain Under the Arabs

In 711 C.E., the Moors, driven by religious fervor, crossed the Straits of Gibraltar. Within four years they had conquered most of Christian Spain. In 755, the city of Cordova became the capital of the Spanish caliphate.

The Moors were tolerant rulers who wanted all their subjects, whether Muslim, Jewish, or Christian, to participate in the life of the new commonwealth they had founded. Although the language of the land was Arabic, and Islam was the religion of the court and the ruling class, opportunity was open to everyone.

The Jews of Spain

The Jews of Spain entered many professions. They worked as farmers and vintners, goldsmiths, tailors, and shoemakers. They were small merchants and large-scale traders. Spanish Jews also entered the sciences, becoming physicians, astronomers, and mathematicians. Many Jews were well-traveled, highly educated, and achieved high positions in the new society. Jews were government officials, and acted as ambassadors and interpreters, carrying out commercial and diplomatic missions in distant lands. Under the Moors a golden age dawned for Spanish Jewry. Schools of Jewish learning were founded. Scholars from Babylon came to Cordova with copies of the Talmud, and taught the Jews of Spain.

Hasdai Ibn Shaprut / ca. 915–970 C.E.

One of the most famous Jewish figures in Cordova was Hasdai Ibn Shaprut. An eminent physician, Hasdai counted the caliph himself among his patients. The caliph considered Hasdai a trusted friend and advisor. Hasdai Ibn Shaprut knew Latin, the language of the learned in Christian Europe, and often acted as the caliph's interpreter. When ambassadors from other countries came to Cordova, he represented the caliph in discussions with them.

As a leading member of the Jewish community of Spain, Hasdai supported the academies, purchase prized copies of the Talmud, and gave fincial assistance to scholars and students, poets and writers.

The Muslim invaders were spurred into battle by the belief that heavenly angels protected them. The Christians adopted St. James, the Moor Killer, as their protector. He was believed to ride a great white horse and wield a deadly sword. This Spanish painting pictures St. James in battle with the Moors.

The Khazars / 8th to 11th C.E.

An ambassador from Persia told Hasdai Ibn Shaprut about the Kingdom of the Khazars on the shores of the Black Sea. This far-off kingdom, ruled by a king named Joseph, stretched to the shores of the Caspian Sea. The Khazars were valiant warriors but they lived as Jews, following the laws of the Torah. Hasdai was greatly excited by this news; could these strange Jews be descendants of the Ten Lost Tribes?

A Letter to King Joseph

Hasdai sent a letter to the Khazar king. It passed through many hands on its journey, and three years went by before Hasdai received a answer. In his reply the Khazar king told Hasdai about his land and people, recounting the story of how they had come to accept the Jewish faith. The Khazars, he explained, were not one of the lost tribes. During the 8th century one of his ancestors, Bulan, had decided to abandon paganism. He invited a Christian, a Muslim, and a Jew to his court, and asked them to describe their respective religions. After hearing their presentations Bulan chose Judaism. Many of his courtiers followed his example, and eventually many other Khazars also became Jews.

The story told by Joseph captured the imagination of many Spanish Jews. It formed the background for one of the classics of medieval Jewish philosophy, Judah Halevi's *Kuzari*.

The Khazar kingdom survived until the 11th or 12th century, when conquering Russian princes destroyed it and scattered its people over the great steppes of Russia.

A letter in Hebrew from a Khazar Jew, dated 950 C.E. It recounts the incidents that led to the conversion of the Khazars to Judaism and events that took place in Khazaria during the 10th century.

The Alcázar castle in central Spain was built by the Moors in the Middle Ages.

Samuel Ibn Nagrela / 993–1056 C.E.

In 1031 C.E. the Cordova caliphate broke up into several smaller Muslim kingdoms. New cities gained importance, among them Malaga, the capital of the caliph of Granada.

The Scholarly Merchant

In the city of Malaga there lived a most unusual man named Samuel Ibn Nagrela (993–1055). Samuel had come to Malaga from Cordova. He earned his living as a spice merchant but was a well-educated man—a philosopher, mathematician, and a fine Hebrew scholar, and knew several languages, including Hebrew, Spanish, Arabic, Greek, and Latin. Many of the city's nobles came to him for advice or to write letters for them.

Even the grand vizier had heard about the scholarly merchant. He so admired Samuel that he appointed him his secretary. When the vizier died, Caliph Badis appointed Samuel in his place. Henceforth, Samuel lived in the palace in Granada. In addition to his other duties, he became the commander of the caliph's army.

Like Hasdai Ibn Shaprut, Samuel Ibn Nagrela always took a deep interest in the Jewish community. He had the most complete and valuable Hebrew library in Spain. He wrote essays on the Talmud, composed poems on both religious and secular subjects, and even worked on a Hebrew grammar.

Samuel, the Prince in Israel

Also like Hasdai, Samuel was very generous. He helped many poets and writers, students and scholars to find work and to support themselves. He aided the charitable collections that supported the poor Jews of Malaga and raised funds for the talmudic academies of Spain, Babylonia, and Palestine. The Jews of Malaga, regarding Samuel Ibn Nagrela as the head of their community, conferred the title of *nagid* ("prince") upon him. Thus he is known in history as Samuel HaNagid.

The Great Mosque of Cordova with its nineteen naves, each with a double layer of vaults, dating from the 8th to 10th century.

Solomon Ibn Gabirol / *ca. 1021–1056*

Among the many writers whom Samuel HaNagid encouraged and supported was Solomon Ibn Gabirol (1020–1057). During his short life Solomon wrote many beautiful poems in Hebrew and Arabic, as well as philosophical works that were widely read by both Jews and non-Jews. He wrote hymns for the Sabbath, festivals, and fast days, many of which found their way into the prayerbook. His most celebrated poem was the ethico-philosophic hymn Keter Malkhut ("Royal Crown"), which became part of the liturgy for the Day of Atonement.

The "Fountain of Life"

Ibn Gabirol's most important philosophical work, *Mekor Hayyim* ("Fountain of Life") explains his personal faith and his view of

The poem "Grief and Desire" by Solomon Ibn Gabirol. The page is from a 12th century manuscript.

God's relationship to the physical world. In the Middle Ages it was translated into Latin under the title *Fons Vitae.* Since it is characterized by a general philosophical approach, with no special emphasis on Judaism, it was long thought to have been written by a Christian philosopher. Ibn Gabirol's authorship was established in 1846 by a scholar doing research on old manuscripts in a Paris library.

A Golden Age

The life of Ibn Gabirol marks a high point in Arabic-Jewish culture, a golden age that began in the 10th century and continued until the 12th. During this period, scholars, poets, scientists, and philosophers flourished in the Jewish communities of Muslim Spain, despite the political strife which surrounded them.

The Court of Lions in the Alhambra of Granada, Spain. This fountain is mentioned in one of the poems of Solomon Ibn Gabirol.

Isaac Hakohen Alfasi / 1013–1103 C.E.

The Jewish academies of Spain produced many talmudic scholars. The founder of the most important Spanish academy was Isaac ben Jacob Hakohen Alfasi (1013–1103). Born in North Africa, Alfasi studied and taught at the academies in Fez and Kairouan for many years. He moved to Spain in 1088 and settled in Lucena, where he became head of the Jewish community and established a center of talmudic learning which became famous throughout the country.

A Guide for Talmud Students

In order to guide judges who had to rule on questions of Jewish law, Isaac Alfasi wrote a great code and commentary on the Talmud in which he concentrated on those parts of the halakhah which seemed most important. This work, the *Sefer Halakhot*, is often referred to as the *Rif*, from the initials *Rabbi Isaac Fasi*. It is still used by students of the Talmud.

Alfasi's method of codifying the laws did not please everyone, however, and many scholars criticized his work. Despite his sharp and precise opinions, Alfasi was a mild and forgiving man. When one of his most bitter opponents was about to die, he made his peace with Alfasi by sending his son to study with the master. Alfasi took the orphaned boy into his own household and taught him together with his own sons and favorite students.

Alfasi's academy in Lucena was attended not only by talmudic scholars but by students who became writers, poets, and communal leaders. Among them were the poets Moses Ibn Ezra and Judah Halevi.

Rabbi Isaac ben Jacob Hakohen Alfasi.

Title page of *Rav Alfas*, the code of Isaac Alfasi. It was printed in 1552, in Venice.

Judah Halevi / 1075–1141 C.E.

To this day, Judah Halevi (1075–1141) is the most beloved of the Spanish-Jewish poets. Born in Toledo, Halevi studied at Alfasi's academy in Lucena, where he received an intensive Hebrew education. A scholar of Arabic literature, he was learned in astronomy and mathematics, and was an eminent physician.

Judah the Poet
Eventually Judah returned to Toledo to practice medicine. Though he was one of the most famous physicians of his day, he felt that he was only a humble assistant to God, the true healer. He wrote:

My medicines are of Thee and bespeak
Thy art—whether good or evil, strong or weak.
The choice is in Thy hands, never in mine:
Knowledge of all things fair and foul, is Thine.
I heal not with some power in me,
But only through the healing sent from Thee.

Although his medical career kept him busy, Judah wrote hundreds of poems of prayer and thanksgiving, many of which are included in the prayerbook. After he married, the light of his life was his one daughter, who became as learned as Rashi's daughters. When she later had a son, she named him in honor of his famous grandfather.

As he grew older, Judah Halevi developed a passionate longing for the Land of Israel and wrote a number of beautiful poems famed as the "Songs of Zion."

The Kuzari
Like most of the other Spanish-Jewish poets, Judah Halevi was interested in philosophy. His most important philosophical work was a book in Arabic called *Kuzari* ("The Khazar"). Based on the letter from King Joseph to Hasdai Ibn Shaprut, it presents a dialogue in which a rabbi explains Judaism to the Khazar monarch. At the end of the book, the rabbi bids farewell to the king and sets out on a journey to Palestine.

Judah Halevi Travels to Israel
In his old age, Judah Halevi set out to see the Land of Israel. His friends tried to dissuade him, for the journey was long and dangerous. But the poet would not change his mind. He crossed the Mediterranean Sea and traveled through North Africa, visiting the Jewish communities along his route. In Fostat (Cairo), Egypt, many urged him to give up the idea of going on to Israel. But the old man was determined to see his dream fulfilled.

The Death of Judah Halevi
Judah Halevi never returned from his journey. When he reached the gates of Jerusalem, he fell upon his knees and kissed the holy ground. As he knelt there, he was trodden to death by the horse of a hostile Arab rider. And so the poet Judah Halevi died—standing at last on the soil of the Land of Israel.

A page from the *Kuzari*. The dialogue form of the work can be seen. On the right side of the page stand the words:

"Said the Kuzari,"

and

"Said the *Haver*" (meaning rabbi), introducing their statements.

Moses ben Maimon / 1135–1204

The Almohades Rule Spain

In the 12th century, when the Almohades, a fanatical Muslim sect from North Africa, invaded Spain, the golden age for Spanish Jewry began drawing to an end.

Unlike Spain's earlier Muslim rulers, the Almohades sought to convert everyone to Islam. They persecuted Jews and Christians alike, forcing them to become Muslims or leave the land. But where could the Jews go? The northern part of Spain was ruled by unfriendly Christian kings. The Crusades, the Christian march to rescue the Holy Land from the Muslims, had begun, and the Jews in Christian lands now faced new dangers.

Moses Maimonides / 1135–1204

Many Spanish Jews set out for North Africa. Among the emigrants was a scholar named Maimon and his family, who fled from Cordova to Morocco. Maimon's son Moses, who was 13 at the time, is today known as Maimonides; in Hebrew he is often referred to as Rambam, an acronym for *Rabbenu Mosheh ben Maimon*.

Maimonides was an eager student, well-versed in Hebrew, the Bible, the Talmud, and other Jewish writings. He also studied mathematics and astronomy, Arabic literature, and the philosophy of the ancient Greeks. Although he had to go to work at an early age, he managed to study medicine and became a skilled physician.

Maimonides Gives Advice

Even as a very young man, Maimonides wrote brilliant books and essays. When the Jews of Morocco were hard-pressed by the Almohades to forsake their religion and become Muslims, they asked Maimonides what they should do. He advised them to leave the place of forced conversion. "Whoever remains in such a place," he said, "desecrates the Divine Name and is nearly as bad as a willful sinner."

The Jews of Morocco heeded his advice. Maimonides himself was forced to leave Morocco for having spoken out so courageously and frankly. He and his family tried to settle in Palestine, but could not do so because conditions there were very unstable.

Portrait of Maimonides.

The autograph of Maimonides.

The gravestone of a grandson of Moses Maimonides, found in Cairo, Egypt. The inscription reads: "This is the grave of David, grandson of Rabbenu the Gaon Moses ben Maimon, Light of the Exile.

Maimonides in Egypt / 1166

Maimonides and his family went to Egypt, where he set up a medical practice in the city of Fostat, near Cairo. His fame spread quickly, and before long he became the personal physician of Sultan Saladin and the royal family. Rich and poor, Jew and Muslim alike, patients of every background consulted him, and the great physician found time to see them all. The wealthy paid for his services, but the poor were treated free of charge.

At the request of the nagid, the leader of the Jewish community, Maimonides also took on the responsibility of providing religious guidance to the Jews of Egypt. He became a greatly beloved teacher. After Sabbath services each week, he gave public lectures on Talmud and Torah.

The Mishneh Torah

Despite his many duties, Maimonides managed to write the most important code of Jewish law since the completion of the Talmud. This great code is called the *Mishneh Torah* ("Repetition of the Torah") or *Yad Hahazakah* ("The Strong Hand").

The *Mishneh Torah* codifies all the laws in the Mishnah and the Talmud, together with the commentaries of the gaonim and the scholars in the generations following them.

Guide for the Perplexed

Maimonides' best-known philosophical work is the *Moreh Nevukhim* ("Guide for the Perplexed"). In it he clearly explains the principles and ideas of Judaism.

Maimonides had to defend himself against critics who disliked his philosophical views and his approach to the Bible. But he was beloved by many scholars and Jewish leaders, and by the many simple people whom he had helped or advised in one way or another. When he died in Fostat in 1204, he was mourned throughout the Jewish world. People compared him to the great leader who had led Israel out of Egypt in ancient times, saying: "From Moses to Moses, there was none like unto Moses."

The city of Cordova, in 1964, honored the memory of Maimonides by erecting a statue in his honor.

The Crusades

The Rise of Islam

Christian Europe felt threatened by the rise of Islam. The leaders of the church supported any effort to drive the Muslims out of Spain and were very concerned about Muslim domination of Palestine. To Christians, as to Jews, Palestine was the Holy Land. They regarded it as holy because it was the place where Jesus, the founder of their faith, had lived and preached.

This painting shows the crusaders besieging Jerusalem. The giant catapult was able to throw a 100-pound stone into the city.

The First Crusade / 1096–1099 C.E.

In 1095 a church council met in the South of France and proclaimed the First Crusade, a holy war to liberate Palestine from the Muslim "unbelievers." Bands of knights and their followers assembled, accompanied by monks, to march to the Holy Land.

As the feeling against unbelievers grew stronger, roused to a fever pitch by inflammatory sermons, a bitter period began for the Jews of Europe. Christian mobs demanded that they accept baptism and massacred those who refused. Several popes issued bulls prohibiting conversion by force, but they did nothing to restrain the clergy from spreading anti-Jewish libels. The accusations resulted in the murder of thousands. When the crusader army captured Jerusalem, it massacred the city's Jewish and Muslim inhabitants.

The Second Crusade / 1146–1147 C.E.

In 1144, during the preparations for the Second Crusade, a monk named Rudolph inflamed the masses in the Rhine valley against the Jews of Germany. People began to believe that killing Jews was God's will. Bernard of Clairvaux, an important Christian leader, rose to the defense of the Jews and tried to stop the campaign against

them. Due to his courageous stand the loss of Jewish life and property was relatively mild in that part of France.

Hospitaller, Teutonic Knight, Templar.
The most dedicated crusaders were members of quasi monastic military orders. The Knights Hospitaller guarded the Hospital of St. John in Jerusalem. The Knights Templar guarded the palace of the king of Jerusalem.

Belvoir Castle was built by the French Knights Hospitaller. It was destroyed in the 13th century by the sultan of Damascus, who was afraid that the crusaders would return. The stone arches are a part of the ruins of Belvoir.

The Jews of York

The Jews of England fared as badly as those on the European continent. The courage of the Jews of York is still remembered. They took refuge in a tower and were besieged by a fanatical mob. Led by their rabbi, Yomtov ben Isaac of Joigny, they chose to take their own lives rather than submit to the forced conversions which the mob had in store for them.

The End of the Crusades / 1189–1192

In 1187, the crusaders were defeated by Saladin, the Egyptian sultan whose court

physician was the great Maimonides. In contrast to the Christian crusaders, Saladin was a tolerant, moderate ruler. Several minor attempts to reconquer Palestine followed, but enthusiasm for Crusades soon petered out.

The Crusades had serious consequences for the Jews of Europe. Even though the Holy Land remained under Muslim domination, life in Europe changed when the crusaders returned. On their journeys, they had learned about distant lands. Many became traders and travelers, taking advantage of the valuable contacts they had established in other lands.

A page from a French history book written in 1337. The painting shows the crusader attack on Jerusalem.

Saladin (1137–1193) captured Jerusalem from the Crusaders. The sultan then summoned the Jews and gave them permission to resettle the Holy City.

This illustration from the *Luttrell Psalter* shows Richard the Lion Heart fighting Saladin during the Third Crusade.

Jewish Changes

Bankers and Moneylenders

In the era before the Crusades, much of the commerce between cities and countries in Europe had been carried out by Jews. But now more non-Jews entered the field.

No longer safely able to engage in large-scale commerce, the Jews were forced to enter other occupations. One area was banking and moneylending, activities in which Christians were forbidden to participate by church law. Jewish bankers and moneylenders managed the financial affairs of princes, bishops, nobles, and kings. But most Jews now had to make their livelihood by keeping pawnshops, lending small amounts of money, or dealing in second-hand goods.

No longer could Jews be craftsmen. The world of medieval Europe had become highly organized and restricted. All craftsmen were organized into guilds, and applicants for membership had to be of the Christian faith. In addition, Jews were no longer permitted to own land or vineyards.

Protectors of the Jews

Some Christian nobles and princes protected the Jews in their territories. This was less often due to tolerance than to the fact that the ruler usually collected higher taxes from the Jews in his domain, who thus were a steady source of income for him.

Since borrowers would sometimes refuse to repay money obtained from Jews, moneylending was often a risky business. In many instances debtors would organize mobs to plunder the Jewish quarter. Often an entire community would be expelled.

Expulsion from England / 1290

King John of England and his son Henry III viewed their Jewish subjects as a source of income. They imposed taxes so severe that

Aaron's house in Lincoln, England.
Aaron of Lincoln (1123–1186) was an English financer whose moneylending clients included bishops, barons and the king of Scotland. Aaron financed the building of ten English churches. After his death, his estate was seized by the king and the state collected the moneys owed to him.

the Jews begged for permission to leave the country. Permission was refused, and further taxes were imposed. In 1290, when the country's 16,000 Jewish inhabitants had nothing left to tax, the entire community was expelled. John confiscated their homes and personal property.

The king furnished ships so that they could return to France, where their families had originated. On the voyage many of the Jewish passengers were robbed and some were thrown to a watery grave in the English Channel. This was the end of English Jewry until the year 1657.

Edict of Louis VII banishing the Jews from France in 1145.

Rabbi Solomon ben Itzhak—Rashi / 1040–1105

A Child Is Born

Despite the grim situation in the Middle Ages, the continuity of Jewish scholarship was assured by the birth of a Jewish child in the year 1040 in the French city of Troyes. This child was destined to become the most popular and important figure of rabbinic Judaism—Rabbi Solomon ben Itzhak, universally known as Rashi (Rabbenu Shlomo Itzhaki).

It is told that Rashi's father was once offered a large sum of money for a valuable gem he owned. He refused to sell it, because he knew it would be used to embellish a Christian religious image. Fearing that the Christians might take the gem by force, he threw it into the sea. As a reward for this deed of loyalty to his faith, he was blessed with a son who would brighten the light of the Torah.

As a youth Rashi studied at the academy of Jacob ben Yakar in Worms, Germany. On his return to Troyes he earned his living from his vineyards, but devoted most of his time to study and writing. Before long his influence radiated throughout the world's Jewish communities.

Rashi's Commentaries

Rashi wrote a commentary to the Torah based on a sound understanding of the plain meaning of the text and of the interpretations incorporated in the talmudic and midrashic literature. Rashi's commentary on the Torah is the most beloved and valuable ever written. In traditional circles, studying Torah without Rashi is virtually unthinkable. Rashi's commentary on the Talmud holds an equally important place. For centuries it has been printed on the same page as the Talmud text, for the convenience of scholars.

The Rashi chapel in the city of Worms, the synagogue where the great commentator worshipped and taught.

Rashi's work of commenting on the Bible and Talmud was continued by his grandsons. The most prominent of them were Rabbi Shemuel ben Meir (1080–1174), known as Rashbam, and Rabbi Jacob ben Meir (1100–1171), known as Rabbenu Tam.

THE RASHI SCRIPT

Mem Sofit	ם	ס	Alef	א	ﬁ
Nun	נ	כ	Beit	ב	ﬧ
Nun Sofit	ן	ן	Gimel	ג	ﬡ
Samech	ס	ﬧ	Daled	ד	7
Ayin	ע	ﬡ	Hay	ה	ﬥ
Fay	פ	ﬢ	Vav	ו	ו
Fay Sofit	ף	ﬧ	Zayin	ז	ﬧ
Tzadi	צ	ﬡ	Chet	ח	ﬨ
Tzadi Sofit	ץ	ﬧ	Tet	ט	ﬡ
Quf	ק	ﬧ	Yud	י	ﬧ
Resh	ר	ﬧ	Khaf	כ	﬩
Sin	ש	ﬧ	Khaf Sofit	ך	ﬧ
Tav	ת	ﬠ	Lamed	ל	ﬥ

Rashi was a prolific scholar and was constantly writing new commentaries. It was difficult and very time-consuming to write using the regular Hebrew alefbet. So Rashi used a cursive script that was much easier and faster to write.

Most of the early commentaries on the Torah and the Talmud were printed in Rashi script.

The Tosafists

Despite the difficult times they had to face, the generations following Rashi continued to study the Talmud and the Torah. The writings of these scholars are called Tosafot ("additions, supplements"), because they were added on to Rashi's commentaries, and the scholars themselves are known as the tosafists.

Rabbenu Tam / 1100–1171

The period of the Tosafot began immediately after Rashi wrote his commentary. Rashi's son-in-laws and grandsons were the first tosafists.

The Tosafot are records of talmudic discussions held primarily in the yeshivot of northern France during the 12th century. Rabbis and students would analyze and discuss talmudic questions. Their conclusions are summarized in notes (also called glosses) printed in all editions of the Talmud on the outer margin opposite Rashi's comments.

The most famous tosafist of the 12th and 13th centuries was Jacob ben Meir, known as Rabbenu Tam, a name which means "Our Perfect Master." Like many other scholars in that era, Rabbenu Tam lost all his belongings in the dark days of the Crusades. Undaunted, he continued with his studies and gave advice and leadership to his fellow Jews. Rabbenu Tam called together a synod or council of rabbis at which rules of conduct and questions of internal government were discussed. The purpose of the synod was to find ways to protect the Jewish community, especially those who were poor and who suffered most from the persecutions.

This synod was followed by other assemblies. The Jews of the Rhineland arranged their communal life as best they could. They helped one another, so that their religious and communal life could continue and those in need could receive help.

Jews were required by law to wear pointed hats and yellow badges.

A page of the Talmud with some of the commentaries. This selection is from tractate Berachot. *Tosafot* means "commentary." The Tosafot are in yellow.

Badges, Blood Libels, and Black Death

The Yellow Badge

In 1215 Pope Urban II decreed that Jews had to wear some means of identification to distinguish them from Christians. From then on, all Jews were required to wear a yellow badge on their garments. In some localities they were also ordered to wear pointed hats.

King Philip the Fair

In 1306, the Jews of France were expelled by King Philip the Fair (1268–1314), who confiscated their money and real estate. But the Christian moneylenders who replaced the banished Jews were so greedy and pitiless that the king soon recalled them to his realm.

Expelling the Jews was financially profitable, however, so the same scenario was played out twice more. After the second time, during the reign of Philip of Valois in 1394, they were not allowed to return. For a thousand years Jews had lived in France. But from then until the time of the French Revolution, there were no Jews in France, except in Avignon, Carpentras, and Cavaillon, which were under the direct rule of the pope, and in Bordeaux and Alsace.

The Black Death / 1348

In the middle of the 14th century, a terrible plague called the Black Death befell Europe, killing millions. A rumor began to circulate that the Jews had poisoned the wells to bring about the disaster. In September of 1348, the Jews of Chillon on Lake Geneva were arrested and forced to confess that they had poisoned wells.

In Strasburg, France, on February 14, 1349, large numbers of Jews were burnt to death. Similar scenes took place in many other areas.

In the German city of Nordhausen, the mob ran wild through the Jewish quarter. To avoid worse tortures, the town's Jews, led by their rabbi, committed suicide by throwing themselves into a fire and burning themselves to death. Scores of persecutions occurred throughout Europe in the wake of the Black Death. Despite efforts by Pope Clement VI to protect them, hundreds of Jewish communities were destroyed and tens of thousands of Jews were slaughtered.

Blood Libels

Exploiting the fear and superstition of the common people, some members of the clergy began spreading a rumor that Jews used the blood of Christian children in their rituals. During Passover, they alleged, Jews had to kill a child and drink its blood or use the blood to make matzot. The first pogrom caused by this libel occurred in 1171 C.E.. The Jews of Blois, in France, were accused of killing a Christian child. In the aftermath, 30 innocent Jews were burned at the stake.

In 1475 the city of Trent, in northern Italy, was the scene of another blood libel incident. The body of a child was found near the home of a Jewish community leader. After questioning under torture, 17 Jews confessed and were executed. As a consequence, no Jews were allowed in Trent until the 18th century. Despite condemnation by the popes, the blood libel accusation has persisted. In 1903, a massacre occurred in Kishinev, Russia, after a blood libel accusation. Forty Jews were killed and hundreds were seriously injured. In 1993 the blood libel once again appeared in Leon, France. The accusation seems to raise its ugly head in different parts of Europe during the Passover season.

Meir of Rothenburg / 1215–1293

Rabbi Meir ben Baruch

One of the great German rabbis of the Middle Ages was Meir ben Baruch of Rothenburg. He was born in 1215 in the city of Worms, where Rashi once had studied. As a young man, Meir was taught by the great rabbis of France and witnessed the burning of the Talmud in Paris in 1242. Returning to Germany, he established a talmudic academy.

In the days of Rabbi Meir, Rudolph I of Hapsburg became the emperor of Germany. Rudolph began his reign as a powerful ruler, endeavoring to control his domain with an iron hand. Previously the nobles had enjoyed complete power over the Jews; now they became subjects of the crown and responsible to the emperor alone. Rudolph raised their taxes and confiscated their property whenever he felt it necessary to punish them.

Rabbi Meir Is Arrested

Many Jews decided to emigrate. A large group, led by Rabbi Meir, set out for Palestine. Rudolph had Rabbi Meir arrested. He felt that the Jews had no right to leave, because they were valuable subjects whose high taxes helped to swell the funds of the royal treasury.

When Rabbi Meir was thrown into prison, the Jews begged the emperor to release him. Rudolph asked them for a large cash ransom.

A Martyr for His People

Rabbi Meir implored his people not to pay the outrageous sum, for he knew that if they did, it would place an even heavier financial burden on the Jewish community. For years he remained in his prison cell. His students often visited him there, bringing letters in which he was asked for legal advice by Jewish courts throughout the land. In 1293 Rabbi Meir died in prison, a martyr by his own choice; he had put the well-being of the Jewish community above his own.

The emperor refused to release the body of Rabbi Meir unless the Jewish community paid a large sum of money for its return. Years later, a German Jew named Alexander Wimpfen paid the ransom on the condition that he would be buried alongside the rabbi. When Alexander died he was buried next to Rabbi Meir.

Flight to the East

The Jews of Germany somehow managed to survive these dark days. Temporary expulsions occurred, but in many instances the Jews were eventually able to return. Doggedly they set about rebuilding their homes, synagogues, and schools, resuming their pattern of study, work, and Sabbath and festival observance.

By the end of the 15th century, new territories in Eastern Europe opened up to immigrants. Poland, Russia, Ukraine, Lithuania, and Hungary all welcomed Jewish settlers from Germany because of their advanced commercial, technical, and industrial skills. The Jewish immigrants who settled in these lands brought their religious heritage, their institutions of learning and self-government, their love of home, and their will to survive.

Tombstone of Rabbi Meir.

Christians in Spain

The Christians Regain Control / ca. 1230

Meanwhile, the Christians were slowly regaining control of Spain. King Alfonso VI of Leon and Castile united the three Christian kingdoms of the north. Alfonso ruled his realm with foresight and tolerance equal to that of the Muslim rulers of an earlier day. Cities again began to flourish. Merchants brought goods from distant lands, and artisans fashioned their wares. Farmers tilled their fields, and shepherds tended their flocks. The Jewish community of Spain benefited from the improved conditions, living in freedom and prosperity.

By the 15th century the rest of Spain had been wrested from the Muslims and the Christian reconquest was practically complete. The church now intensified its efforts to convert the country's Jews.

Christianity Debates Judaism

The friars of the Dominican order were charged with the task of winning over the Jews. One of them, a convert from Judaism named Pablo Christiani, was very eager to make converts. He persuaded King James I to hold a public debate at Barcelona. In the debate Pablo would pit his arguments for Christianity against the arguments of a learned rabbi.

This altar relief shows the forced conversion of Jewish women. The women were forced to choose between conversion and exile.

Bullfighting was a popular Spanish sport. This 13th century painting shows the spectators throwing darts called banderillas at the bull.

Spain enjoyed an economic boom and the affluent public demanded luxuries. Enterprising merchants, some of them Jews, established trading companies which imported luxuries from the Orient, India, Russia, Venice and France. These Spanish women are shopping for luxuries at a country fair.

Nahmanides / 1194–1270

Rabbi Moses ben Nahman

The rabbi chosen to defend Judaism in the debate before the king's court and many high-ranking church dignitaries was Moses ben Nahman (1194–1270), also known as Nahmanides and as Ramban (from Rabbi Moses ben Nahman).

Nahmanides was Spanish Jewry's most important scholar and rabbinic leader. He earned his living as a physician and served as rabbi of the town of Gerona. His responsa on questions of Jewish law were circulated to Jewish communities throughout the world.

The Debate

Nahmanides stood undaunted before the court and the king to face the fanatical Pablo and the other Dominican friars. In the debate Pablo tried to prove that Jesus was the Messiah, citing isolated talmudic statements to support his claim. Nahmanides easily refuted him. The statements quoted by Pablo, he explained, were legends and tales that had no bearing on what Jews believed. The important part of the Talmud was its legal portion, the halakhah, and that contained nothing whatsoever to support Pablo's arguments.

Nahmanides asked a very important question. How, he inquired, could Jesus have been the Messiah if wars were still being waged between nations? The coming of the Messiah was supposed to usher in an era of peace and goodwill, but this had still not come to pass.

The wisdom of the aged Nahmanides impressed the king, who adjourned the debate without declaring Pablo the victor. On parting with Nahmanides, the king gave him a generous gift. Nahmanides published the text of the debate. When Pablo heard about this he reported it to the

Nahmanides' synagogue in Jerusalem. From the *Casale Pilgrim,* a 16th century guide to the holy places of Palestine.

king. Again Nahmanides was summoned. This time he was sentenced to two years in exile.

Nahmanides in Israel

Nahmanides went to Palestine. He was grieved by the state of the Jews there. Wars and invasions had impoverished the Jewish communities of the Holy Land. Schools no longer existed, and only a very few synagogues still stood intact.

The aged scholar devoted the last years of his life to the Jewish community in Palestine. He built a synagogue in Jerusalem and opened a school. Scholars and students gathered around him. Before his death, Nahmanides could see the results of his work. The spiritual life of the Jews in Palestine had been enriched and rejuvenated through his efforts.

Seal of Nahmanides found near the city of Acre.

The Kabbalah

A system of thought based on mysticism began to gain ground among Spanish Jewry. This system, known as Kabbalah, sought hidden meanings in the Torah that would explain difficult religious problems. Among these were such questions as how the world could have been created out of nothingness, how God, who is perfect, could enter into relations with imperfect human beings, and where evil came from.

Moses de Leon / 1250–1305

The most important kabbalistic work was the Zohar ("Brilliance"), a mystical commentary on the Torah that was supposed to have been written in Palestine in the 2nd century C.E. by Simeon bar Yohai.

The work remained unknown until the 13th century, when a copy was found by a man named Moses de Leon.

Most scholars believe that Moses de Leon himself was the author of the Zohar, although it may contain some material dating back to Simeon's time. The book de Leon produced was full of strange and wonderful ideas. It explained how God had created the world through ten steps and suggested how man could purify his soul and rise to a higher level of understanding. For adherents of Kabbalah it seemed to be an inexhaustible source of profound knowledge about spiritual matters of compelling importance.

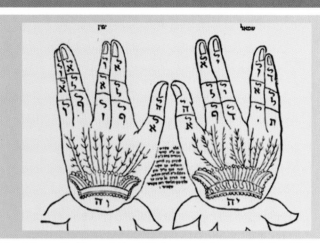

Most Jews believed that Hebrew letters and the Hebrew language were sacred, since they were used by God to create the world. The kabbalist Abraham Abulafia (1240–1300) believed that combinations of letters could help an individual achieve prophetic vision and knowledge of God.

The above is a kabbalistic drawing showing the channels of divine emanation and letter combinations in the form of hands.

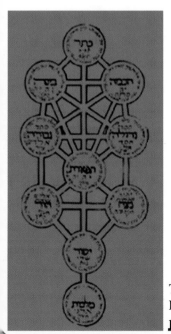

The ten mystic spheres of God. From a book of Kabbalah printed in Mantua, Italy, 1562.

Title page of the first edition of the Zohar, Mantua, 1558.

The Marranos

Samuel Abulafia / 1320–1361

Christian Spain was divided into two kingdoms, Aragon and Castile. Under King Pedro the Cruel, who ruled in Castile, a Jew named Samuel Abulafia became the royal treasurer. Abulafia helped build the Sinagoga del Transito in Toledo, a magnificent synagogue which is still in use as a church.

When Henry of Trastamara, Pedro's half-brother, revolted, the Jews of Castile fought valiantly for their king. Pedro was defeated, however, and his half-brother ascended to the throne of Castile and Leon as Henry II.

Baptism or Death

Henry hated the Jews because they had fought against him. During his reign, zealous monks incited mobs to sack Jewish homes throughout Castile. For the first time, Jews in Spain were required to wear the yellow badge, a humiliation already familiar to Jews in the rest of Europe. A wave of anti-Jewish feeling and riots swept through Spain. The Jews were given a choice—baptism or death. Unlike their coreligionists in northern Europe, many of them chose baptism and became Christians. Some of Spain's most respected Jewish leaders were among the baptized. Frequently entire communities converted together. The baptized Jews, officially known as New Christians, were never fully accepted into Spanish society, as shown by the fact that they were usually called Marranos, which means "pigs."

The New Christians

The Old Christians of Spain detested the New Christians. Competition was one of the main reasons. Now that the Jews were Christians, they were able to compete openly in fields that had been closed to them when they were Jews. In addition, many Spaniards feared that the new converts were not sincere Christians.

Throughout the 15th century riots broke out—not against Jews but against Marranos. The government was forced to ban Marranos from holding public office. Many Marranos remained Jews at heart, or turned to Judaism again when the Christians did not treat them fairly. They attended church and had their children baptized, but began to practice their old faith in secret. They met in secret places to hold services. They observed the festivals and the Sabbath, and studied the Torah.

Isabella and Ferdinand witness the conversion of a Jew. Note that the kneeling Jew has crossed his arms into the shape of a cross.

The Inquisition

Ferdinand and Isabella

When Isabella of Castile and Ferdinand II of Aragon married in 1469, the two great kingdoms of Spain were united. At that time three different religions were still practiced in the land, Christianity, Judaism, and Islam. But Queen Isabella yearned to make Spain an all-Christian nation. She delegated great powers to the dreaded Inquisition, headed by the infamous Tomas Torquemada, and many of its victims were burned at the stake.

Torquemada

Torquemada, the soul of the Inquisition, was determined to rid Spain of the Marranos. He published a series of instructions called *Constitutions* for the guidance of judges. In it he detailed how accused New Christians were to be tortured and how to dispose of their properties.

Persecution of the Marranos

Distrusted by the Old Christians, the New Christians were constantly watched by spies and informers. Anyone suspected of secretly practicing Judaism was arrested and brought before the Inquisition, which confiscated their property and subjected them to torture to make them confess. Many of the Marranos brought before the Inquisition "repented." Many others, however, bravely refused, remaining loyal to the religion of their ancestors even though this meant a terrible death by burning at the stake.

It gradually became clear to Isabella and Ferdinand that the continued presence of Jews in Spain was one of the factors causing Marranos to backslide from Christianity. They decided to give the Jews of Spain a simple choice: either become Christians or leave the country.

The infamous Torquemada.

New Christians Fight Back

The New Christians did not surrender without a fight. Influential Marranos protested to the king and the pope. But Ferdinand was resolute in his determination to use the Inquisition to acquire the property of the victims.

Juan Perez Sanchez and Juan de Abadia organized a team to assassinate Pedro Arbues, the chief inquisitor of Aragon. The assassination was successful, but it brought a vast number of new victims into the hands of the inquisitors. More than 200 supporters and conspirators were rounded up, dragged through the streets of Saragossa, and hanged.

Juan de Abadia, the chief conspirator, was caught, but escaped torture by killing himself in prison.

The city of Granada in Southern Spain was the last outpost of Moorish control. It was captured by the Christians in 1492. This painting shows Ferdinand and Isabella triumphantly entering the city.

The Expulsion from Spain / 1492

Isaac Abrabanel / 1437–1508

Isabella and Ferdinand had several trusted Jewish advisors. Among them were Isaac Abrabanel, Luis de Santangel, Gabriel Sanchez, and Abraham Senior. Abrabanel was not only an excellent financier but a wise man whose opinion was valued at court. In addition, he was a

Isaac Abrabanel

scholar, philosopher, and author, and a leading member of the Jewish community. When the king and queen issued the order expelling the Jews from Spain, Isaac Abrabanel asked them to rescind it, offering a large sum of gold and silver if they did so. But his plea was in vain. Had he chosen, Abrabanel could have stayed in Spain as an exception to the royal edict because his services were appreciated and needed. He chose instead to leave, casting his lot with his friends and brethren, the Jewish people.

The Jews Leave Spain

The date of the expulsion on the Hebrew calendar was the 9th day of the month of Av in the year 1492 C.E. This was the very same day on which the First Temple had been destroyed by the Babylonians in 586 B.C.E. and the Second Temple had been destroyed by the Romans in 70 C.E.

Each destruction had been followed by a period of exile. Now, Jews already living in exile from their true homeland in Israel had to go into a third exile, from the adopted land in which they had once been so happy. Once again, the Jews of exile were being forced into exile. Spanish Jewry, which had lived through a golden age unsurpassed in the history of the Jewish dispersion, was now coming to an end.

Everything had to be left behind. Jews who had property traded it for sturdy traveling clothes. Precious jewels were exchanged for food for the long and perilous journey. The exodus was so terrible a catastrophe that it even shocked Spanish and Italian witnesses who detested Jews. Many of the exiles died from the hardships of the journey or were robbed and murdered. All suffered from a terrible sense of shock and dislocation.

King Ferdinand, Queen Isabella, and Torquemada, the Grand Inquisitor, kneel in prayer.

Christopher Columbus

On August 3, 1492, just one day after the expulsion took place, the *Nina*, the *Pinta*, and the *Santa Maria*, under the command of Christopher Columbus, set sail westward across the Atlantic Ocean in search of a sea route to India. Columbus had received much of the money needed to finance his expedition from Marranos. Many of his maps were made by Jews who knew the art of map-making and the routes across the great seas. It is said that some members of his crew were Marranos. Indeed, the famous navigator himself may have been of Jewish origin, according to some scholars.

Christopher Columbus was convinced that he could reach the Orient by sailing westward. He failed to identify America as a new continent, thinking it was part of India.

As his three ships hoisted anchor that day, Columbus made a note in his log of the Jewish refugee ships which he sighted as he began the journey which was to alter the map of the world.

A map from a Catalonian atlas by the Spanish-Jewish cartographer Abraham Cresque, 1375.

The expulsion of the Jews from Spain marked the end of a memorable epoch. The journey of Columbus, however, signified a beginning, for it set the stage for the birth, centuries later, of a new nation in a faraway land, where Jews would live in freedom.

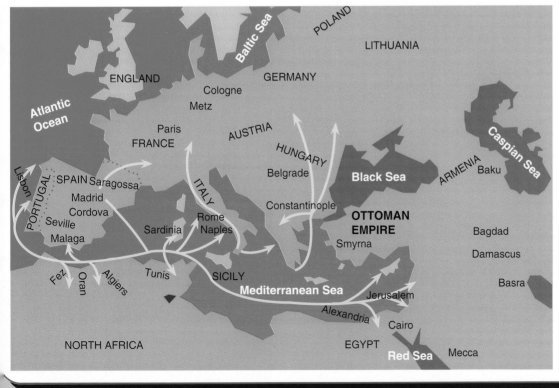

The expulsion from Spain in 1492. The map shows how the first exiles went to Portugal and southern Italy; persecution followed and many fled eastward to countries of the Ottoman Empire.

Timeline—The Age of Europe Begins

JEWISH HIGHLIGHTS

Age of Gaonim
7th–11th century

Karaites
founded 762 C.E.

Khazars
8th–11th century

Golden age of Spain
9th–12th century

Moses ben Maimon
1135–1204

Christian Crusades
11th–13th century

JEWISH EVENTS • PERSONALITIES • LITERATURE • HOLIDAYS

Age of Gaonim	Karaites	Khazars	Golden age of Spain	Moses ben Maimon	Christian Crusades
Saadia Gaon	Saadia Gaon	Khazar kingdom destroyed in 11th century	Moors conquer Spain 715 C.E.	Mishneh Torah	Jews massacred
First Siddur	Anan ben David		Hasdai Ibn Shaprut	Guide for the Perplexed	Saladin defeats Crusaders
Sura	Hananiah		Samuel Ibn Nagrela		
Pumpeditha	Gaonim		Solomon Ibn Gabirol		
Halakhah			Isaac Alfasi		
Responsa			Judah Halevi		
Bustanai					
Masorah					

WORLD HISTORY

Age of Gaonim	Karaites	Khazars	Golden age of Spain	Moses ben Maimon	Christian Crusades
Muslims	Babylonia	Russia	Arabs	Morocco	France
Khosru			Moors	Egypt	Germany
			Caliph of Cordova	Fostat	England
					Italy

Timeline—The Age of Europe Begins

JEWISH HIGHLIGHTS

English Jews
10th–12th century

Rashi and family
11th–12th century

European expulsions
13th–15th century

Christians conquer Spain
12th–15th century

New Christians
14th–15th century

Spanish Expulsion
1492

JEWISH EVENTS • PERSONALITIES • LITERATURE • HOLIDAYS

▷ English Jews expelled. 1290

▷ Bible and Talmud commentaries

▷ New script

▷ Rabbenu Tam

▷ Tosafists

▷ Synods

▷ Yellow badges

▷ Black Death

▷ Blood libels

▷ Meir of Rothenburg

▷ Economic restrictions

▷ Christian/Jewish debates

▷ Nahmanides

▷ Inquisition

▷ Auto-da-fé

▷ Marranos

▷ Samuel Abulafia

▷ Isaac Abrabanel

▷ Tisha Be-Av

▷ Torquemada

▷ Columbus

▷ Sephardim

WORLD HISTORY

▷ England

▷ King John

▷ King Henry

▷ France

▷ Troyes

▷ Rhineland

▷ Popes

▷ France

▷ Rhineland

▷ Spain

▷ King Alfonso VI

▷ King James I

▷ King Pedro

▷ King Ferdinand

▷ Queen Isabella

▷ Portugal

The Jews Leave Spain

Where were the Spanish refugees to turn? England had expelled her Jews; so had France. In German lands Jews fared badly, subject to suspicion, persecution, and expulsion. Many Jews from Germany had already sought new homes in the east, in Poland and Lithuania. Some German Jews, especially those who were scholars and successful merchants, had gone to Italy, where Jewish communities were said to prosper under the influence of the free spirit of the new learning encouraged by the Renaissance.

A Haven in Portugal

Closest to Spain was the kingdom of Portugal. Here, for a short span of time, many of the refugees found a haven. They had to pay a poll tax but were permitted to practice their trades and crafts. Their new home was of short duration, however. The king of Portugal had married Princess Isabella of Spain, the daughter of Ferdinand and Isabella. They had agreed to the marriage only on the condition that Portugal become a Christian country free of all heretics and Jews.

In 1497, the king of Portugal the country's Jews expelled. However, when they reported to the port cities, they were all forcibly converted to Catholicism.

New Homes in Muslim Countries

Some of the Jews driven out of Spain went to North Africa. There they found new homes in Tunis, Fez, and Algiers, or in the great cities of Cairo and Alexandria in Egypt. Many other Spanish Jews found a refuge in the Ottoman (Turkish) Empire, which welcomed them because of their skills and treated them tolerantly. Under Ottoman rule, many became merchants, scholars, and physicians. Sultan Bajazet, pleased with his new subjects, reportedly said, "How can you call Ferdinand of Aragon a wise king, when he has impoverished his land and enriched ours?"

"The Dutch Jerusalem"

So many Portuguese and Spanish Marranos settled in Holland that the city of Amsterdam was often called the Dutch Jerusalem. This name was coined in 1596, when a group of Portuguese Marranos there returned to Judaism in a solemn, public ceremony. From that time on, Amsterdam was a great center of European Jewry.

1492 EXPULSION
New Homes for Spanish Jews

To Turkey	90.000
To Holland	25.000
To Morocco	20.000
To France	10.000
To Italy	10.000
To America	5000
Total emigrated	**160.000**
Died while seeking new home	20.000
Baptized, remained in Spain	50.000

The old synagogue of the Sephardic community in Amsterdam, Holland. The reader's desk is in the center of the synagogue.

Index

A

Aaron (high priest), 13, 17, 18, 21, 26
Aaron of Lincoln, 146
Abadia, Juan de, 155
Abaye (amora), 122—123
Abba Arikha (amora), 120
Abdul Malik Ibn Marwan (caliph), 127
Abner (Saul's general), 32
Abrabanel, Isaac (advisor of Ferdinand and Isabella), 156
Abraham (patriarch), 9—11, 19, 49, 62
   in Islam,, 126, 129
Abu Bakr (caliph), 128
Abulafia, Samuel (treasurer of Pedro the Cruel), 154
Abyssinia (Ethiopia), 70, 125
Academies and schools
   Babylonia, 116, 120—121, 122, 132, 138
   France, 147, 148
   Germany, 147, 150
   North Africa, 136, 140
   Palestine, 85, 102-103, 106, 116, 119, 138, 152
   Spain, 136, 138, 140, 141
Achish (Philistine king), 31
Acre (Akko), 152
Adar
   14th of, 71
   Kallah month, 120
Aegean Sea, 25
Aelia Capitolina (Roman Jerusalem), 109
Afghanistan, 74
Africa, 90
Ahab (king of Israel), 41, 42, 44
Ahasuerus (Persian king), 70—71
Ahavah Rabbah (prayer), 120
Ahaz (king of Judah), 42, 47, 50
Ahaziah (king of Israel), 44
Ahriman (Zoroastrian god), 121
Ahura Mazda (Zoroastrian god), 121
Ai (Canaanite city), 20
Akiva (tanna), 106, 108, 110, 111
Alcazar (Spanish castle), 137
Alenu (prayer), 121
Alexander Jannai (Hasmonean ruler), 85, 89
Alexander the Great (Macedonian king), 65, 74, 75, 107
Alexandria (Egyptian city), 74–75, 76, 79, 87, 160
Alfasi, Isaac (talmudist), 140, 141
Alfonso VI (Spanish king), 151
Algiers (North African city), 160
Allah (God, in Islam), 126, 128
Almohades (Moorish sect), 142
Alsace (French region), 71, 149

Altars, 34
Amalekites (desert tribe), 15
America, 157, 160
Amidah (prayer), 121
Ammon/Ammonites, 29, 59, 65
Amon (king of Israel), 53
Amoraim (sages of Gemara), 113, 116, 122
Amos (prophet), 46, 49
Amram (father of Moses), 12
Amsterdam (Dutch city), 160
Anan ben David (Karaite leader), 133
Anathoth (Jeremiah's town), 58
Angels, 11, 17
Antigonus (Macedonian general), 74, 89
Antioch (Syrian city), 80
Antiochus III (Seleucid king), 78
Antiochus IV (Seleucid king), 78, 80, 82, 84
Antipater (father of Herod), 87
Antonia (Judean fortress), 91
Antony, Mark (Roman leader), 88–89
Aphek, battle of, 26
Apocrypha, 53, 77
Apostoli (emissaries), 115
Apries (Egyptian king), 59
Aqueducts, 87
Arabia, 74, 90, 126–127
   Jews of, 125, 128
   in Solomon's time, 34
Arabic (language), 127, 128, 134, 139, 141
Arab Legion, 103
Arad (Negev town), 34
Aragon (Spanish kingdom), 154, 155
Aram (Syria), 40, 43, 44, 45, 47
Aramaic (language), 69, 77, 111, 113
Arbues, Pedro (Spanish official), 155
Aristobulus I (Hasmonean prince), 85
Aristobulus II (Hasmonean prince), 86
Ark of the Covenant. See Holy Ark
Armenia, 97
Arms and armor, 14, 15, 25, 30, 31, 81, 82, 97, 100, 103, 108, 117
Arslan-Tash (archaeological site), 43
Artaxerxes I (Persian king), 66, 67
Ashdod (Philistine city), 25
Ashkelon (Philistine city), 25
Ashtoreth (Canaanite goddess), 28
Ashurbanipal (Assyrian king), 30, 54, 55
Asia Minor, 80
Assimilation, 21, 70–71, 75
Assyria
   decline and fall, 54, 56
   and Israel, 44, 45, 46, 47, 48
   and Judah, 50, 52–53, 54, 55
   Ten Lost Tribes, 48, 49, 63
   mentioned, 40, 94
Astarte (Canaanite goddess), 27, 43
Athaliah (queen of Judah), 44
Athens (Greek city), 71
Atonement, Day of (Yom Kippur), 139
Augustus (Octavian) (Roman emperor), 88,

89, 94
Av, 9th of, 59, 98–99, 156
Av bet din (Sanhedrin leader), 92
Avdat (archaeological site), 118
Avignon (French city), 149
Avot (Mishnah tractate), 92

B

Baal (Canaanite god), 27, 28, 41, 42, 49
Babylonian Empire, 49, 52, 55, 56, 58, 62, 74
Babylonian Exile
   deportations from Judah, 57, 59, 118
   life in exile, 57, 61–62
   return from, 60, 62, 63, 66
Babylonian Jewry
   and Arabs, 132, 133
   Aramaic, 111
   center of learning, 92, 111, 116, 120, 122, 124, 132
   Karaism, 133, 134
   and Parthians, 121, 122
   and Persians, 70, 121
   prosperity of, 118, 119
   self-government of, 119, 120
   spiritual center, 118, 132, 134
Babylonian Talmud, 116, 122, 124
Badis (caliph), 138
Bajazet (Ottoman sultan), 160
Balkans, 97
Banking and moneylending, 146
Baptism, 94, 154
Barak (Israelite general), 22–23, 31
Bar'am (archaeological site), 110
Barcelona (Spanish city), 151
Bar Kochba (Judean leader), 108–109
Baruch (Jeremiah's servant), 58
Bathsheba (David's wife), 33
Belshazzar (Babylonian prince), 61
Belvoir Castle, 145
Ben Asher (Masorete), 135
Benjamin (tribe), 28, 38
Ben Naphtali (Masorete), 135
Berachot (Mishnah tractate), 148
Bernard of Clairvaux (Christian leader), 144
Bertinoro, Obadiah (Mishnah commentator), 113
Betar (Judean fortress), 109
Bet Hamikdash (Holy Temple), 34
Bethel (Judean city), 22, 28, 39, 46
Beth Haran (Israelite city), 34
Beth-Horon (Israelite city), 36, 82, 83
Bet Hillel (House of Hillel), 93
Bethlehem (Judean city), 30, 90, 91
Beth-She'an (Judean city), 31, 110
Beth She'arim (academy), 110, 111, 112

Bezalel (craftsman), 17, 83
Bible
     canonization and standardization of, 77, 135
          Christian, 104
          divisions of, 77
          in Jewish life, 77
          Karaite view of, 133
          translations of, 69, 79, 134
          See also Torah
Biran, Abraham (archaeologist), 32
Black Death, 149
Black Sea, 137
Blois (French city), 149
Blood libel, 149
Bnai Mikra (Karaites), 133
B'ne B'rak (Judean city), 106
Bordeaux (French city), 149
Britain (Roman province), 107, 109. See also England
Bulan (Khazar king), 137
Bullfighting, 151
Bull god, 39
Burning Bush, 13
Bustanai (exilarch), 132
Byzantium/Byzantine Empire, 33, 115, 118, 125

C

Caesar, Julius (Roman ruler), 86, 87, 88
Caesarea (Galilean city), 81, 87, 88, 90, 95, 107
Cairo (Egyptian city), 141, 143, 160
Cairo Genizah, 134
Caleb (Israelite leader), 18
Caliphs/Caliphate, 128, 132, 136, 138
Cambyses II (Persian king), 64
Canaan/Canaanites
     God's promise regarding, 10
     Israelite conquest, 19, 20, 21, 22-23, 31
     Israelite spies, 15, 18
     and patriarchs, 10–11
     tribal land portions, 21
Capernaum (Galilean city), 26, 95
Carchemish, battle of, 44, 56
Carmel, Mount, 42
Carpentras (French city), 149
Carthage (North African city), 136
Cartographers, 157
Casale Pilgrim (medieval book), 152
Castile (Spanish kingdom), 151, 154, 155
Catacombs. See Tombs/tombstones
Cathedra (chair) of Moses, 92
Cavaillon (French town), 149
Censorship, of Mishnah, 114
Chaldeans, 55
Cherubim, 17
Children of Israel, 11
Chillon (French town), 149
Christiani, Pablo (monk), 151, 152

Christianity
     and Islam, 142, 144
     and Judaism, 115, 151, 152
     Khazars, 137
     origins of, 94, 104
     in Roman Empire, 115, 118
     See also Conversion; Crusades
Chronicles, Books of, 77
Circumcision, 107
City of David, 67
Clement VI (pope), 149
Cleopatra (Egyptian queen), 87
Coins, 65, 66, 84, 97, 98, 101, 102, 109, 115
Columbus, Christopher, 157
Constantine II (Roman emperor), 115
Constantine the Great (Roman emperor), 115
Constantinople, 115, 118, 134
Conversion
     to Christianity, 144, 145, 151, 152, 154, 160
          to Islam, 142
          to Judaism, 69, 137
          of Khazars, 137
          See also Marranos
Copper, 34, 35
Cordova (Spanish city), 136, 138, 142, 143
Craft guilds, 146
Cresque, Abraham (map-maker), 157
Crete, 25
Crusades, 33, 142, 144—145, 146, 148
Cyprus, 107
Cyrene (North African city), 107
Cyrus the Great (Persian king), 61, 62, 64
     tomb of, 63

D

Dacia (Romania), 107
Daf Yomi (Talmud study), 116
Damascus (Syrian city), 45, 46, 86, 127, 145
Dan (tribe), 25, 39
Daniel (prophet), 61
Daric (Persian coin), 65
Darius I (Persian king), 64, 65, 67, 70
Darius III (Persian king), 75
Date palm, 125
David (king of Israel)
     anointed by Samuel, 30
     as musician and poet, 30, 31, 32, 33
     Citadel of, 33
     dynasty. See David, House of
     length of reign, 37
     military exploits, 11, 30, 32–33, 36
David, House of
     exilarchs, 119, 132, 133
     rulers of Judah, 37, 38, 39, 40, 44, 59
     rulers of Judea, 63
Dead Sea, 20, 91, 109
Dead Sea Scrolls, 50, 60, 94, 96

Debates
     Jewish-Christian, 152
     Jewish-Christian-Muslim, 137
Deborah (prophetess), 22, 23, 31
Decapolis (league of cities), 90
de Leon, Moses (author of Zohar), 153
Delilah (Philistine woman), 25
Deuteronomy, Book of, 54
Diaspora (Dispersion), 74, 79, 92
Dominicans (monastic order), 151, 152
Dura-Europos (archaeological site), 27, 70

E

Eastern Europe, 150
Ecclesiastes, Book of, 35, 77
Edom/Edomites, 47, 59, 64, 84
Eglon (Canaanite city), 20
Egypt
     Exodus from, 12–15, 18, 43
          and Israel/Judah, 34, 38, 39, 47, 52, 55–56, 58, 59
     Jewish revolt in, 107
     Karaites, 133
     in patriarchal era, 12
     Ptolemaic, 74, 75, 78
     in Roman era, 86, 87, 97, 107
     under Muslim rule, 128, 143
     mentioned, 40, 90, 92
Ekron (Philistine city), 25
Elam/Elamites, 54, 57
Elazar (son of Aaron), 21
Eleazar (uncle of Bar Kochba), 108
Eleazar ben Yair (Zealot leader), 100, 101
Elephants, 82
Eli (high priest), 26
Eliakim (royal official), 56
Eliezer (Abraham's servant), 10, 106
Eliezer Maccabee, 81
Elijah (prophet), 42, 43
Elisha (prophet), 42–43, 44
Elul (month), 120
Emissaries, 118, 132
Emmaus (Syrian camp), 82
England/English Jewry, 97, 145, 146, 160
Ephraim (tribe), 21, 22, 37, 38
Ephron the Hittite (seller of Cave of Machpelah), 10
Esarhaddon (Assyrian king), 53
Essenes (sect), 94, 96
Esther (Persian queen), 70, 71
     Book (Scroll) of, 71, 77
Ethiopia (Abyssinia), 70, 125
Ethnarchs (Roman officials), 87, 94
Euphrates River, 9
Exilarchs (Babylonian Jewish leaders), 119, 122, 132
Exodus, 13–15, 18, 43
Expulsions
     England, 146, 160
     France, 146, 149, 160

Portugal, 160
  Spain, 59, 155, 156, 157, 160
Ezion-Geber (Red Sea port), 34, 35
Ezra (exile leader), 24, 67, 68, 69
  Book of, 62, 77

F

Ferdinand (Spanish king), 154, 155, 156, 160
Fertile Crescent, 10, 11
Fez (North Africa city), 140, 160
First Revolt (against Rome), 90, 91, 96–97, 98, 100–101, 102
Five Books of Moses. See Torah
Flamethrowers, 117
Florus (Roman official), 96
Fons Vitae (Ibn Gabirol), 139
Fortresses, 90, 91, 100–101
Fostat, 141, 143
Four Gospels, 104
France, 97, 144, 149, 160
French Jewry, 132, 147, 149
Fund-raising, 115, 118, 138

G

Galilee
  academies, 110, 111
  anti-Roman resistance, 88, 94, 97, 98, 115
  Herod as governor, 87
  oldest Jewish village, 107
  Sea of, 95
  synagogues, 26, 92, 110
  mentioned, 92, 107
Gamaliel II (tanna), 105
Gamaliel the Elder (tanna), 105, 111
Gamaliel V (patriarch), 116
Gamaliel VI (patriarch), 118
Gaonim, 124, 132, 134
Gath (Philistine city), 25, 31, 32
Gaul (Roman province), 107. See also France
Gaza (Philistine city), 25, 84
Gemara, 116, 124
Gerizim, Mount, 64
Germany/German Jewry, 107, 144, 148, 149, 150, 160
Gerona (Spanish city), 152
Gezer (Israelite town), 36
Gezer Calendar Stone, 24
Gibeah (Saul's fortress), 29
Gideon (judge), 24
Gihon River, 52
Gilboa, Mount, 31, 111
Gilgal, 29
Gladd Chronicle (Babylonian tablet), 55
"God-fearers" (non-Jews interested in Judaism), 76

Golden calves, 39
Goliath (Philistine giant), 30
Goshen (Egyptian region), 12
Granada (Spanish kingdom), 138, 139, 155
Great Assembly (Sanhedrin)
    democratic/representative body, 84, 85, 77, 105
      functions of, 77, 85, 92, 103
      and Hasmoneans, 84, 85
      and Herod, 88, 92
      leaders of, 92, 93, 105, 110
      opposed revolt against Rome, 94, 96
      membership and organization of, 92, 103
      mentioned, 102, 118
Great Sanhedrin. See Great Assembly
Great Synagogue. See Great Assembly
Greece, 71, 74, 80, 90, 97
Greek culture and language. See Hellenism
"Grief and Desire" (Ibn Gabirol), 139
Guide for the Perplexed (Maimonides), 143
Gymnasia, 79

H

Hadrian (Roman emperor), 107, 108, 109, 115
Haftarah (prophetic readings), 105
Haggai (prophet), 64
Halakhah (Jewish law), 16, 113, 122, 132, 140, 152
Halevi, Judah (philosopher-poet), 137, 140, 141
Haman (Persian official), 71
Hananiah ben David (exilarch), 133
Hanina (tanna), 111
Hannah (Samuel's mother), 26
Hanukkah, 83
Haran (Mesopotamiam region), 9, 10, 55
Hasdai Ibn Shaprut (advisor of caliph), 136, 137, 138, 141
Hasidim (opponents of Hellenists), 78, 79, 80, 96
Hasmoneans (Maccabee family), 80, 89
Hazor (Canaanite city), 21, 36
Heber (Jael's husband), 23
Hebrew
    diminishing knowledge of, 79, 111, 134
    grammar and punctuation, 135, 138
    modes of writing, 29, 68, 133, 147
    mystical aspects, 153
    poetry in, 134, 139
    Samaritan Torah in, 64
    Torah and Mishnah in, 69, 77, 111
Hebrews, origin of name, 9
Hebrew University, 109
Hebron (Judean city), 10, 11, 32
Hegira (Muhammad's flight), 126
Hellenism, 64, 78, 79
Heller, Yomtov Lipman (German rabbi), 113

Henry II (Spanish king), 154
Henry III (English king), 146
Herod Antipas (tetrarch of Galilee), 94
Herodium (fortress), 90, 91
Herod the Great
    building projects, 33, 90, 91, 100
    cruelty, 88, 89, 90
    governor of Galilee, 87, 88
    king of Judea, 89, 90–91
    and Rome, 88–89
    mentioned, 78, 92, 94
Hezekiah (king of Judah), 52–53, 88, 94
High priests, 74, 77
    garments of, 17
    Hasmonean, 84, 85, 86
    Roman appointees, 86, 92
    See also names of high priests
Hilkiah (high priest), 54
Hillel II (nasi), 115, 116
Hillel the Elder, 92–93, 105, 112, 119
    House of, 93
Hiram (king of Tyre), 34, 35
Hittites (Canaanite people), 20
Holland, 160
Holy Ark
    David brings to Jerusalem, 33
    descriptions of, 17, 26
    Philistines capture, 26, 27
    portability pf, 17, 18, 20
    at Shiloh, 21
    in Tabernacle, 17, 18, 35
    in Temple, 35
Holy of Holies, 17
Hosea (prophet), 46, 49
Hoshea, (king of Israel) 47
Hospital of St. John (Jerusalem), 144
Huldah (prophetess), 54
Hungary, 150, 150
Hyksos (conquerors of Egypt), 12
Hyrcanus (high priest), 86, 87, 88, 89

I

Ibrahim ibn Yusuf al-Israili (Yemenite Jew), 125
Idol worship
    Canaanite, 21, 22, 27, 28, 39, 42–43
    Egyptian, 56
    Greek, 79, 80
    Islam condemns, 126
    in northern kingdom, 40–41, 42, 43, 46, 49
    in southern kingdom, 45, 50, 53, 54
    in time of judges, 22, 27, 28
Idumea, 84, 84, 87, 94
India, 70, 90, 107, 128
Inquisition, 155
Iran, 74
Iraq, 74
Isaac (patriarch), 10, 11, 19, 49
Isabella (Spanish queen), 154, 155, 156, 160

Isaiah (prophet), 50–51, 52, 53
  Book of, 51
Isaiah Scroll, 50, 94
Ishbosheth (Saul's son), 32
Ishmael (Abraham's son), 126, 129
Ishtar (Babylonian goddess), 70
Ishtar Gate (Babylon), 60
Islam
  and Christianity, 142, 144
  and Jews, 127, 136, 139, 141
  and Khazars, 137
  origins and beliefs of, 126
  in Spain, 136, 139, 142
  spread of, 127, 128
Israel, Children of, 11
Israel, Kingdom of
  and Assyria, 44, 45, 46, 47–48
  and Egypt, 38, 39
  fall of, 48, 51, 63
  founding of, 38
  idol worship in, 39, 40–42, 46
  instability of, 41
  and Judah, 39, 40, 44
  prophets in, 41–43, 46, 49
Israel, origin of name, 11
Israel, State of, emblem, 83
Israel Museum, 94
Issus, battle of, 75
Italy, 149, 160
Ivrim (Hebrews), 9

Jabbok River, 11
Jabesh-Gilead (city in Gilead), 29, 31
Jabin (Canaanite king), 22, 23
Jacob (patriarch), 10, 11, 12, 19, 49
Jacob ben Asher (Masorete), 135
Jacob ben Meir (tosafist), 147, 148
Jacob ben Yakar (Rashi's teacher), 147
Jaddua (high priest), 74
Jael (Kenite woman), 23
James, St. (Spanish warrior), 138
James I (Spanish king), 151
Jebusites (Canaanite tribe), 20, 32
Jehoahaz (king of Israel), 45, 56
Jehoash (king of Israel), 45, 46
Jehoiachin (king of Judah), 56, 57, 119
Jehoiada (high priest), 44, 45
Jehoiakim, (king of Judah) 56
Jehoram (king of Israel), 43, 44, 45
Jehu (king of Israel), 43, 44, 45
Jeremiah (prophet), 58, 59
Jericho (Judean city), 20
Jeroboam I (king of Israel), 36, 38, 39, 40, 41, 46, 48
Jeroboam II (king of Israel), 46
Jerusalem
  under Arabs, 127, 129, 132
  and Assyrians, 52, 53
  and Babylonians, 57, 59, 63
  Bar Kochba, 108

as capital, 33, 40
under crusaders, 144, 145
David's conquest of, 11, 32, 67
exiles rebuild, 66–67
fortifications of, 33, 52, 66, 91
and Hadrian, 107, 108, 109
Israel Museum, 94
and Jesus of Nazareth, 95
and Judah Halevi, 141
and Maccabees, 82
Meah Shearim, 103
and Muhammad, 127
as religious center, 92, 104
and Romans, 86, 98, 100, 102, 103
and Saladin, 145
and Shishak, 39
synagogues and holy places of, 92, 103, 152
Jerusalem Talmud, 116
Jesse (David's father), 30
Jesus of Nazareth, 95, 104, 115, 144, 152
Jethro (Moses' father-in-law), 13
Jewish law. See Halakhah
Jewish War (Josephus), 99, 101
Jezebel (queen of Israel), 41, 42, 44
Jezreel, plain of, 22, 42, 55
Joab (David's general), 32
Joash (king of Judah), 44
Job, Book of, 77
Jochebed (Moses' mother), 12
John (English king), 146
John Hyrcanus (Hasmonean ruler), 84, 85
John (Yohanan) of Giscala (Zealot leader), 97
John the Baptist (wandering preacher), 95
Jonathan (Saul's son), 30, 31
Jonathan Maccabee, 81, 83, 84
Jordan (kingdom), 11, 84
Jordan River, 10, 20, 42, 94
Joseph (Jacob's son), 12, 36, 111, 137
Joseph bar Ham (amora), 122
Josephus Flavius (historian), 98, 99, 101, 102
Joshua (biblical leader)
  chain of tradition, 92
  conquered Canaan, 20-21, 22
  scouted Canaan, 18
  succeeded Moses, 19
Joshua (tanna), 106
Josiah (king of Judah), 53, 54–55, 56
Judah (tribe), 30, 32, 37, 38, 94
Judah, Kingdom of
  and Assyrians, 50, 52–53, 54
  and Babylonians, 49, 56–59, 60
  Davidic dynasty, 38, 40
  Deuteronomic revival, 54
  and Egyptians, 39, 55
  prophets in, 50, 51
  relations with Israel, 39, 44, 47, 50
  See also Judea
Judah ben Ilai (tanna), 110
Judah HaNasi (Judah the Prince), 110–113, 114, 116, 120, 124
Judah IV (amora), 116

Judah Maccabee, 81, 82, 83, 98
Judea
  and Alexander the Great, 74
  First Revolt, 96, 97, 98, 99, 102
  and Herod, 89, 90, 92
  and Maccabees, 82, 84
  and Parthians, 89
  and Romans, 86, 87, 92, 94, 108
  Second Commonwealth, 63, 78
  Second Revolt, 109
  and Seleucids, 78
  See also Judah, Kingdom of
Judges (biblical leaders), 22, 24, 26
Julian the Apostate (Roman emperor), 115
Jupiter (Roman god), 81, 107

Kaaba (Muslim shrine), 129
Kabbalah (mystical lore), 153
Kadesh-Barnea (Sinai oasis), 15
Kairouan (North African city), 136, 140
Kallah months, 120, 124
Karaites (anti-talmudic sect), 133, 134
Karnak (Egyptian temple), 38
Kenites (tribe), 13, 23
Keter Malkhut (Ibn Gabirol), 139
Ketubot (Mishnah tractate), 113
Ketuvim (section of Tanak), 77
Khazars (Black Sea tribe), 137
Khorsabad (Assyrian city), 51
Khosru I (Parthian king), 124
Khosru II (Parthian king), 124
Kilayim (Mishnah tractate), 114
Kings, Book of, 34
Kingship, 24, 28, 36
Kiryat Arba (Judean town), 11
Kishinev (Russian town), 149
Kishon River, 22, 23
Kislev, 25th of, 83
Knights Hospitaller (crusader order), 144, 145
Knights Templar (crusader order), 144
Kohanim (priests), 17
Kohelet, Book of, 35
Koran (Muslim Scripture), 128
Korazim (Galilean town), 92
Kuzari (Halevi), 137, 141

Laban (uncle of Jacob), 10
Lachish (Judean city), 20, 49
Lake Geneva, 149
Lamentations, Book of, 60, 77
Leah (matriarch), 11
Leon (French city), 149, 151
Levi (tribe), 12, 21
Levites, 28, 61, 65, 67
Lithuania, 150, 160

Louis VII (French king), 146
Lucena (Spanish city), 140, 141
Luttrell Psalter (medieval hymnal), 145
Lyres, 57

M

Macalister, R. (archaeologist), 24
Maccabees, tombs of, 81
Macedonia, 74, 80
Machpelah, Cave of, 10, 11
Maimonides, Moses (Rambam), 142, 143, 145
Malaga (Spanish city), 138
Mamre (site near Hebron), 10
Manasseh (Judean king), 53
Map-making, 157
Marah (spring), 15
Marathon, battle of, 71
Marcus Aurelius (Roman emperor), 111
Marduk (Babylonian god), 70
Mari (Mesopotamian kingdom), 9, 10
Mariamne (wife of Herod), 89
Mark (New Testament author), 104
Marranos (New Christians), 154, 155, 157
Mar Samuel (amora), 116, 120–121
Martyrdom, 145, 149
Masada (fortress), 91, 100–101
Masorah/Masoretes (standardizers of Bible text), 135
Mattathias (father of Judah Maccabee), 80, 81
Matzot (unleavened bread), 14, 149
Mecca (Arabian city), 125, 126, 127
Medes (Iranian people), 54, 55, 56, 57, 61
Medina (Arabian city), 127
Megiddo (Palestinian city), 36, 41, 46, 55, 56
Megillah (Scroll of Esther), 71
Meir (tanna), 112
Meir of Rothenburg (German rabbi), 150
Mekor Hayyim (Ibn Gabirol), 139
Menachem (king of Israel), 40, 47
Men of the Great Assembly, 92
Menorah, Temple, 83, 98, 99
Merneptah (Egyptian king), 13, 14
Meron, Waters of, 20
Mesopotamia, 9, 40, 47, 89, 97, 107
Messiah, 43, 94, 95, 108, 152
    in Islam, 127
Meturgeman (translator), 69
Micah (prophet), 51
Michal (Saul's daughter), 30, 33
Midian/Midianites, 13, 24
Midrash, 68
Mikvot (ritual baths), 91
Miriam (Moses' sister), 15, 18
Mishnah
    Abaye, 122
    Akiva, 106, 111
    Bertinoro, 113
    divisions, 112
    Gemara, 116, 124

illustrated, 113, 114
Judah HaNasi, 111, 112, 124
Maimonides, 143
Oral Tradition, 68, 92, 106, 111, 112
Rav, 120
mentioned, 93, 143
See also Talmud
Mishneh Torah (Maimonides), 143
Moabite Stone, 41
Moab/Moabites, 41, 43, 44, 59, 65
Modin (Judean town), 80, 81, 83
Moneylenders, 149
Moors (North African people), 136, 138, 155
Mordecai (Esther's uncle), 70, 71
Moreh Nevukhim (Maimonides), 143
Morocco, 142
Moses
    birth and early life of, 12–13
    in chain of tradition, 68, 92
    chair of, 92
    death of, 19
    in desert, 17–19, 26
    and Exodus, 13–15
    Five Books of, 77
    Islamic view of, 126
    name of, 13
    Song of, 15, 125
    status of in Jewish history, 19, 112, 143
    and Tabernacle/Ark, 17, 26, 27
    and Ten Commandments, 16, 27
    and Torah, 16, 77
Moses ben Asher (Masorete), 135
Moses ben Nahman (Nahmanides), 152
Moses Ibn Ezra (Spanish poet), 140
Mount of Olives, 111
Mount Zion, 35, 50
Muhammad (Islamic prophet), 126–127, 128
Murashu and Sons, 60, 61
Musical instruments, 30, 32, 57
Mysticism, 153

N

Nabatea (region in Jordan), 84
Nablus (Palestinian town), 64
Nabonidus (Babylonian king), 62
Nabopolassar (Babylonian king), 55
Naboth (victim of Ahab), 42
Nagid (prince), 138
Nahmanides, Moses (Spanish rabbi), 152
Nahum (prophet), 54
Naphtali (tribe), 22
Naqshi-i-Roustem (Persian site), 67
Nasi (head of Sanhedrin), 92, 93, 110, 118
Nathan (prophet), 33
Nazis, 71
Nebo, Mount, 19
Nebuchadnezzar (Babylonian king), 56, 57, 59, 98, 118, 119
Necho (Egyptian king), 55, 56

Negev (Palestinian region), 34
Nehardea (academy), 116, 120, 121
Nehemiah (postexilic leader), 67, 68
    Book of, 77
Nero (Roman emperor), 97, 98
Neviim (division of Tanak), 77, 105
New Christians, 154, 155
New Testament, 104
Nimrud (Assyrian city), 45, 47
Nineveh (Assyrian city), 49, 53, 54, 55
Nippur (Babylonian city), 60, 61
Nonbelievers, under Islam, 129
Nordhausen (German city), 149
North Africa
    Arab conquest of, 128
    Jewish community of, 132, 136, 142
    Karaites in, 133
    refuge for Spanish exiles, 160
    under Romans, 97
    Torah study in, 92, 140
    See also Moors
Northern kingdom. See Israel, Kingdom of
Nubians, 14

O

Octavian. See Augustus
Oholiab (craftsman), 17
Oil, miracle of, 83
Olives, 93
Omar (Muslim caliph)
    conquests of, 128
    Mosque of, 127
    Pact of, 129
Omri (Israelite king), 41, 48
    House of, 41, 42, 44
Onkelos (translator), 69
Ophir (Arabian region), 34
Oral Tradition
    chain of tradition, 68, 92
    Karaite view of, 133
    organizing and writing down of, 106, 111-112
    Pharisee view of, 85, 93, 95
    Sadducee views of, 85, 133
Oslo Agreement, 11
Othman (Muslim caliph), 128
Ottoman Empire, 157, 160

P

Paganism, 22, 79
Pakistan, 74
Palestine, origin of name, 25
Palestinian Authority, 11
Palestinian Targum, 69
Papyrus (paper), 13
Paris (French city), 150
Parthian Empire, 89, 107, 119, 121
Passive resistance, 102
Passover (Pesach)

blood libel, 149
  matzot, 14
  Seder, 43, 125
  mentioned, 95, 100
Patriarchate, 110, 118, 124
Paul of Tarsus (Christian leader), 104
Pawnshops, 146
Pedro the Cruel (Spanish king), 154
Pekah (Israelite king), 47
Pekahiah (Israelite king), 47
Peki'in (Galilee village), 107
Perez Sanchez, Juan (Marrano resister), 155
Persecutions
  and Black Death, 149
  and Crusades, 144
  in England, 145, 146
  in France, 146
  in Germany, 148, 149, 150, 160
  in Muslim countries, 141, 142
  in Persia, 71, 121, 125
  in Rome, 115
  in Spain, 142, 151, 154, 155, 160
  in Yemen, 125
  See also Expulsions; Yellow badge
Persepolis (Persian city), 66, 70, 121
Persia
  and Alexander the Great, 74, 75
  and Arabs, 128
  conquers Babylon, 61, 62
  Jews of, 70–71, 122
  under Parthians, 89, 90, 92, 121
  and Purim, 70–71
  and returning exiles, 62, 64, 66, 67
  and Yemen, 125
  mentioned, 57, 124
Persian Gulf, 10
Pesach (Passover), 14, 105
Peshat, 122
Petra (city in Jordan), 84
Pharaoh
  of Exodus, 12, 13
  of Joseph, 12
  See also Egypt
Pharisees (religious movement), 85, 86, 92, 94, 95, 102
Phasael (Herod's brother), 87, 89
Philip (Macedonian king), 74
Philip of Valois (French king), 149
Philip the Fair (French king), 149
Philistia/Philistines, 25, 26, 27, 29, 30, 31, 32, 47, 57
Philosophers, 134, 138, 139, 141, 143
Phinehas (high priest), 21
Phoenicia/Phoenicians
  and Ahab, 41, 44
  and Assyria, 47
  and Babylon, 57, 59
  and Persia, 66
  religion of, 41, 46
  and Solomon, 34, 35
  writing system of, 68

Physicians, 136, 141, 142, 143, 152, 160
Pilgrimages
  from Diaspora, 84, 99
  to Jerusalem, 21, 22, 26, 33, 105
  Muslim, 127, 129
Poets, 129, 134, 138, 139
Poland, 150, 160
Poll tax, 129, 160
Pompeii (Roman city), 75, 78
Pompey (Roman general), 86, 87
Pontius Pilate (Roman official), 95
Popes (heads of Catholic Church), 149, 155
Portugal, 51, 157, 160
Praetorian Guard, 97
Prayerbook. See Siddur
Priests, 17, 21, 28, 35, 61, 65, 67, 85
Procurators, 87, 94, 96
Promised Land, 9, 10, 18
Prophets, 33, 40, 46, 49, 50, 51, 54, 61, 64, 68, 126
  books of, 77, 105
  chain of tradition, 92
  Muhammad, 127
Proverbs, Book of, 35, 77
Psalms, Book of, 33, 60, 61, 77
Ptolemy I (Egyptian king), 74
Ptolemy II Philadelphus (Egyptian king), 76
Ptolemy IV (Egyptian king), 76
Ptolemy V (Egyptian king), 78
Ptolemy XII (Egyptian king), 87
Pul (Assyrian king), 47
Pumpeditha (academy), 120, 121, 122–123, 124, 132, 133
Purim (holiday), 71

Q

Qumran (site near Dead Sea), 94, 96

R

Rabbenu Tam (Jacob ben Meir), 147, 148
Rabbi, title, 103
Rabina (amora), 124
Rachel (matriarch), 11, 106
Ramah (site near Bethel), 22
Rambam (Maimonides), 142
Rameses II (Egyptian king), 12, 13, 14
Rameses III (Egyptian king), 25
Rashbam (Shemuel ben Meir), 147
Rashi (Solomon ben Itzhak), 141, 147, 148, 150
Rashi script, 147
Rav (amora), 116, 120, 121, 122
Rava (amora), 122, 123
Rav Alfas (Alfasi), 140
Rav Ashi (amora), 124
Red Sea, 14, 34
  parting of, 15

Rehoboam (king of Israel), 37, 38, 39
Renaissance, 160
Rephidim (region in Sinai), 15
Resh galuta (exilarch), 119
Responsa (answers to legal questions), 132, 134, 150, 152
Rhineland (German region), 144, 148
Richard the Lion Heart (English king), 145
Rif (Alfasi), 140
Ritual objects, 83
Roman Empire
  and Judea, 92, 94, 95, 107
  conquers Asia Minor and Syria, 80, 86
  and Christianity, 115, 118
  citizenship of, 87
  civil war, 86, 87
  division of, 118
  Jewish revolts against, 96–97, 107, 108–109
  treaties with Maccabees, 83, 84
Rosh Hashanah (New Year), 121
Royal marriages, 33, 34, 36
Rudolph (monk), 144
Rudolph I (German emperor), 150
Rules of Accents (Jacob ben Asher), 135
Russia, 137, 150, 150
Ruth, Book of, 77

 S

Saadia Gaon (philosopher), 134
Sabbaths and festivals
  Karaite observance of, 133
  Marrano observance of, 154
  synagogue service, 68, 139, 143, 150
  Torah reading, 16, 17
Sacrifices
  discontinued during Roman siege, 98
  heathen, 80
  meaningless if unaccompanied by justice, 46, 51
  Muslim condemnation of, 126
  in northern shrines, 39, 46
  resumed under Bar Kochba, 108
  in Tabernacle, 17, 21
  in Temple, 34, 35, 65, 98
Sadducees (religious movement), 85, 133
Saladin (Egyptian sultan), 33, 143, 145
Salamis, battle of, 71
Salome Alexandra (Judean queen), 85, 86
Samaria (capital of Israel)
  destruction of, 48, 51, 57
  founded by Omri, 41
  under Romans, 94
  mentioned, 39, 44, 46, 63
Samaritans, 48, 63, 64
Samson (judge), 25
Samuel (prophet), 26–29, 30, 36, 116, 120–121
  Books of, 77